THE
COOK'S BOOK
OF™
UNCOMMON RECIPES

What the reviews said about Barbara Hill's other books...

THE COOK'S BOOK OF ™ESSENTIAL INFORMATION

ASSOCIATED PRESS "...packed with information to chart a course through buying, storing, cooking and eating food ... finally here is what you need to know, in one place ... no need to search through every cookbook you own..."

CHICAGO TRIBUNE "We liked (it) so much that we immediately stamped in "property of the test kitchen" so it will not disappear."

LOS ANGELES MAGAZINE "Finally, the answer to your cooking questions ... in this handy volume."

MILWAUKEE SENTINEL "(It) is a lot of book for the money. It offers loads of information..."

THE COOK'S BOOK OF ™INDISPENSABLE IDEAS

MIAMI HERALD: "(It) follow up her *Cook's Book of ™Essential Information* (and) addresses kitchen topics from spices and herbs to wine to losing weight to 200 ways to save time and money. Both are small treasurers."

American Library Association BOOKLIST: "...follows up ... with this new volume of helpful hints and data for the home cook. A valuable reference tool ... availab   ⌐nsonable price."

LUBBOCK AVALANCHE-JOURNAL: " beneficial to all cooks, regardless c

THE SARATOGIAN: "Barbara Hill ... has pu. every cook needs into this gem."

THE

COOK'S BOOK

OF™

UNCOMMON RECIPES

A Kitchen Companion

by
Barbara Hill

Sumner House Press
Kennewick, Washington

First printing 1989

Although the author and publisher have exhaustively researched all sources to ensure the accuracy and completeness of the information contained in this book, we assume no responsibility for errors, inaccuracies, omissions, or any inconsistency herein. Any slights of people or organizations are unintentional. Readers should use their own judgement and/or consult their personal physician or a nutritional counselor for specific application of the nutritional information included.

Since this book was written primarily for readers whose native language is English, and since the diacritical (accent) marks that appear on foreign words do little to assist these readers with pronunciation, the accent marks have been intentionally omitted from the book.

Library of Congress Card Number: 87-60667 CIP participant
ISBN: 0-940367-14-9

Printed in the United States of America

Table of Contents

Arranged in alphabetical order according the most important word in the title, you will find recipes for all kinds of uncommonly good food from appetizers to desserts. This arrangement is designed for browsing. To find a specific recipe, or a recipe calling for a specific ingredient, check in the index.

Have you ever had bread that was heavy, or muffins that had tunnels, or gummy rice, or a souffle that didn't rise? Everyone has something go wrong occasionally. In this section you can learn why these things happen and how to avoid them.

When you are looking for a specific recipe, turn here first. You will find entries by recipe title, the kind of dish it is, and important ingredients.

Special thanks to the friends who tested these recipes in their own kitchens, who made suggestions and comments to make the recipes more usable, and who were a great support group:

Margaret Dzwilewski
Trish Fleischer
Michelle Gerdes
Lynn Hawley
Carolyn Lutton
Sue Ronniger
Edythe Varoz
Kate Welch
Herb and Dorothy Wright

Thanks also to Loretto Hulse who edited the recipes.

A final thank you to three people who started contributing to this book while I was in the cradle, my mother Florence Smith Welch, my father Toby Welch, and my grandmother Grace Roberts Smith. They were all terrific cooks. They taught me very early in my life that good food on the table was the result of caring for people, loving to cook, and respecting food products. I'm sorry they are not still here to see what they have helped me to do.

Introduction

What is an uncommon recipe?

That is the question I asked myself as I went through my notebooks, index cards, and various slips of paper in preparing to write this book.

The first conclusion that I came to is that an uncommon recipe is one that a cook would not be able to find easily, and that probably would not be found in "standard" cookbooks.

The second conclusion I reached is that the recipes should be those that I feel are "uncommonly" good, practical, and reliable.

I believe the recipes in this collection are both of these things.

All of the recipes have been tested in at least two kitchens... kitchens very much like yours, not elaborate "test kitchens" staffed by professional home economists. Much as I admire and certainly respect those well-trained professionals, I believe that they approach food preparation from a different point of view than those of us who simply want to cook good meals for ourselves and our families and friends.

The people who tested these recipes are cooks just like you and me. People who used their own measuring devices, their own pans and ovens, and brought to their evaluation of the recipes their own family's likes and dislikes.

The comments they made were very valuable in putting together the final version of the recipes, many of which have come to me in what might be called "casual" ways... through notes made when my Mother or Grandmother cooked, from phone conversations, and from sketchy instructions jotted down on a three by five card.

My special thanks go to each of these test cooks for their very special help.

The recipe section of the book is in an alphabetical arrangement generally, but not always, by the main ingredient of the recipe. (All of the chicken breast recipes are together, for instance.) This is different from most cookbooks which arrange recipes by category (all of the appetizers together, all of the soups, and so forth). Most of us who enjoy cooking also enjoy cookbook browsing and it seemed to me that this arrangement might lead to some serendipitous discoveries.

The index at the end of the book allows you to find any recipe quickly whether you are looking by title, category, or important ingredient.

A word or two about some aspects of the recipes...

Butter/Margarine

In many recipes you will see "butter/margarine" indicated as an ingredient. This means that you can use either butter or margarine and the recipe will turn out well. Your choice will probably be made based on whether or not you are concerned with controlling intake of saturated fats.

Butter, of course, is a saturated fat and for people for whom cholesterol is a problem, it should probably be avoided or at least limited. On the other hand, there are characteristics of real butter that I believe cannot be duplicated by a substitute. You have to make your own decision.

In some of the recipes either butter or margarine is particularly specified. In those instances I believe that you will be happiest with the results if you use the one called for.

Flour

While all-purpose flour may be used in any of the recipes calling for flour, there are instances where it will not work as well as the cake flour or bread flour that is specified.

"All-purpose" flour is made by combining flours made from hard wheat and soft wheat. Each has its own characteristics which make it ideal for certain kinds of baking, but when combined you do not get the best of both. You might say that all-purpose flour is a compromise and, like all compromises, something is sacrificed by all parties to reach a common ground.

Yeast bread is best when made from hard wheat flour. Hard wheat contains more gluten, and it is this plant protein substance that provides the structure that allows the bread dough to raise. Most bread flours also contain the additive potassium bromate which helps the gluten to do its job and produce a well-shaped loaf with a fine grain. Bread flour is sometimes called "baker's flour".

Cakes and other more fragile baked goods leavened with baking powder, on the other hand, are more satisfactory when made with cake flour which is milled from soft wheat. Soft wheat flour produces a softer and more consistent crumb size because of its lower gluten content.

Cooking Oils

In recipes that call simply for "oil", any mild vegetable cooking oil such as corn, sunflower, or a blend can be used.

For sauteing, you may find that you prefer an oil that can reach a higher temperature without smoking, such as peanut oil.

Olive oil has a distinctive flavor. Where it is called for it is used for its flavor as well as its characteristics as a cooking oil. If you don't like the taste, use something else but I personally don't believe the dish will be as good.

Measurements

In this book you will find ingredient amounts specified by the standard abbreviations: tsp for teaspoon, tbsp for tablespoon, and so forth.

Home-canning Recipes

There are a number of "food preservation" recipes... jams, jellies, and so forth, included in this collection. I have only included those that are safe to process in a boiling water bath and you will find quite explicit directions for processing in "Canning Using a Boiling Water Bath Process".

When you prepare food for long term storage, it is very important to carefully follow directions because unless preservation is done properly the food can spoil. On the other hand, what is required for successful food preservation using the boiling water bath method is so little, and the results are so satisfying, that I have always felt it is worth the trouble.

Why Things Go Wrong

The book concludes with a section on "why things go wrong". We all have had it happen... a recipe that should turn out well but doesn't. Perhaps in this list you will find the reason why, so that it won't happen again. If you have had a problem that you don't find explained on this list, write to me in care of my publisher. If I can find an explanation and a solution, I'll let you know what it is.

Similarly, if you have been looking for a recipe and haven't been able to find it, write and let me know what it is. Perhaps I can find your "uncommon" recipe for you... perhaps you will find it in this book!

Apple Cake

You use fresh apples to make this moist, fragrant cake. It's not terribly sweet and very good with a generous dollop of whipped cream. It's a nice addition to a brunch buffet too.

Yield: 10-12 servings
Oven setting: 325 degrees Fahrenheit

- **2 cups cake flour** (all-purpose flour can be used but cake flour is better)
- **1 1/2 cups sugar**
- **1 1/2 tsp baking soda**
- **1 tsp ground cinnamon**
- **1/2 tsp ground nutmeg**
- **1/2 tsp salt**
- **2 eggs**
- **1 1/2 pounds cooking apples** (4-5 medium)
- **1/2 cup chopped walnuts**
- **1/2 cup raisins** (golden raisins look best)
- **1/2 cup softened butter/margarine**
- **Powdered sugar**

Use shortening to grease a 9x13-inch baking pan and dust it with flour.

Combine flour, sugar, soda, cinnamon, nutmeg and salt in a large bowl.

Beat eggs together lightly. Pare and finely dice the apples. Add apples to dry ingredients. Add nuts, raisins, soft butter/margarine, and eggs. Mix until just combined, do not over mix. Turn the batter, which is quite thick, into your prepared baking pan, spreading it out so that there is an even layer of batter. Bake 1 hour or until it begins to pull away from the sides of the pan slightly and center is firm.

Turn the cake out of pan onto a plate and then on to a cooling rack so that the top is up. When the cake has cooled slightly, dust the top with powdered sugar. Cut into squares to serve.

Home-canned Apple Pie Filling

Apple pie is certainly a universally popular dessert. The convenience of having the filling on your shelf and ready to use is hard to over-estimate. This is also a great money saver because commercially prepared pie fillings are not inexpensive. A full quart of fillings gives you a generous filling for your pie unlike the amount in a typical purchased can. This filling is great for apple turnovers.

Yield: 2 quarts

1 1/2 cups sugar
2 1/2 cups water
3 pounds apples (see suggested varieties below)
4 tsp commercial ascorbic or citric acid (*Fruit Fresh* is one)
6 tbsp cornstarch
1/4 tsp salt
1/2 cup lemon juice (if using Delicious apples)

(See "Canning Using Boiling Water Bath Processing" on page 29 for complete information on how to process the Apple Pie Filling for long term storage.)

Dissolve 1 cup of the sugar in 2 cups of water by bringing to a boil and stirring until crystals are dissolved. Cool the syrup and add the ascorbic or citric acid and stir well.

Wash, peel and slice the apples into the syrup. The slices should be about 1/4 inch thick for best results. Bring the apples to a boil, lower the heat and cook for 5 minutes. Remove from the heat, stir the mixture and allow to rest for 15 minutes.

While the apples are resting in the syrup, combine the remaining 1/2 cup of sugar, the cornstarch and the salt. Stir in 1/2 cups water and form a smooth paste. Slowly add this paste to the apple mixture and stir just enough to mix thoroughly. (If you are using red or golden Delicious apples and need the extra tartness, this is the time to add the lemon juice.)

Bring the apple filling to a boil and cook for just 1 minute more. Immediately fill the quart jars with the hot filling and process in a boiling water bath for 40 minutes. (See page 29.)

This is a reasonably sweet filling, if you prefer it less or more sweet, you can increase or decrease the sugar by about 1/4 cup in either direction.

It is tempting to make a large batch of this filling, but you are best advised to make two quarts at a time so that the fruit will cook evenly and the thickening will be properly distributed. If you want to do more than 2 quarts at a time, prepare two separate pans of the filling at the same time.

Well-flavored varieties of apples such as Jonathan, Mackintosh, Granny Smith, or Gravenstein are good for this. You can also use either red or yellow Delicious, but they need the extra lemon juice to enhance their flavor.

Apricot Butter

You know how good apple butter is... apricot butter is even better! The slightly tangy flavor of the apricots sharpens the spicy sweetness. This is good not only as a jam, but also as a topping for vanilla ice cream or custardy bread pudding. The length of time you cook it will determine the thickness, although it does thicken a little more in the jar.

Yield: About 4-5 half-pint jars

- **3 pounds very ripe apricots**
- **2 tbsp lemon juice**
- **3 cups sugar**
- **2 tbsp lemon juice** (additional)
- **1 tsp ground cinnamon**
- **1/2 tsp ground allspice**

(See "Canning Using Boiling Water Bath Processing" on page 29 for complete information on how to process the Apricot Butter for long-term storage.)

To make apricot puree:
Place apricots, a few at a time, in your blender or food processor and process into a smooth puree. Add 2 tbsp lemon juice to keep the puree from darkening. If time is short, you can put the puree in the freezer in air-tight containers and make the apricot butter later. Three pounds of apricots should make 1 quart of puree.

To make apricot butter:
Use 1 quart of apricot puree and mix it with the sugar and remaining 2 tbsp lemon juice, cinnamon and allspice in a large pan. Bring the mixture to a boil and cook until thickened. It is necessary to stir the mixture just about constantly as it will stick to the bottom of the pan and burn if you don't. The length of time it takes to thicken will depend partly on how juicy the fruit was but it will take no less than 20 minutes and probably no more than about 45 minutes. To judge thickness, spoon a small amount onto a cold dish and see if it sets up to your satisfaction (personal preference enters into this too... some people like it thicker than others).

When apricot butter is ready immediately pour it into the hot jars, place lids on top and tighten rings around. Process for 5 minutes in a boiling water bath. (See page 29.)

This recipe can be doubled or even tripled to make a larger batch.

Artichokes with Sour Cream and Ham Sauce

This attractive dish can be used either as a first course appetizer, or as a light luncheon on its own. To use as an appetizer, look for small artichokes and leave only a few rows of "leaves", for a luncheon dish you'll probably want a fairly good sized artichoke for each person.

Yield: Sauce amount serves 4 as an appetizer, 2-3 as a light meal

1 fresh artichoke for each serving
1/4 cup lemon juice
1 tsp salt
1 cup sour cream
1/2 cup mayonnaise
1/2 tsp worcestershire sauce
1/2 tsp garlic powder
1/2 tsp salt
1/4 tsp pepper (white pepper if possible)
1 cup finely minced ham

Prepare artichokes by cutting off and discarding stem and top third of artichoke. Trim off the coarse bottom leaves and the tips of the remaining leaves. Place with bottoms down in a pan with enough boiling water to cover to which lemon juice and 1 tsp salt has been added. Cook 30-40 minutes or until tender.

Turn upside down on cake cooling rack to drain. While still warm, gently but firmly press down the leaves until the choke at the center is revealed. Trim out this portion and the yellow leaves near it. Put opened artichoke on a plate and weight it down with a second plate to flatten slightly.

Make sauce by combining the rest of the ingredients and mixing well. Divide the sauce among the artichokes. Serve on a bed of mixed greens (lettuces and/or spinach). Garnish with paprika and parsley.

Bagels (Water bagels)

There are basically water bagels and egg bagels, but loads of variations on those two basic themes. All manner of things, onions, poppy seeds, sesame seeds and so forth can be added to the batter or scattered on top. This is a recipe for bagels without added eggs... water bagels.

Bagels are unusual in that they are parboiled before they are baked. The result of this somewhat peculiar procedure is a baked product that is firm, chewy and shiny. When you form the rings, be sure to pinch the two ends together firmly enough that the ring will stay intact through the cooking processes.

Yield: 24 bagels
Oven setting: 400 degrees Fahrenheit

- **1 pkg dry yeast**
- **1 1/2 cups warm water**
- **2 tsp salt**
- **3 tbsp sugar**
- **6 cups bread flour** (use all-purpose flour only if it is all you can find)
- **1 tbsp sugar** (for cooking water)

Dissolve the yeast in the water. Add the salt and sugar and stir until dissolved. Stir in the flour. Knead dough for about 10 minutes. (If kneading by hand, turn out onto a lightly floured board or counter. If kneading in your mixer or food processor, follow manufacturer's directions for kneading bread dough.)

Oil a large bowl and place the kneaded dough in it. Turn the dough to bring up the oiled side. Place the bowl in a warm place for 20 minutes to allow it to rise slightly.

Punch the dough down and turn out onto a lightly floured board. With your rolling pin, flatten the dough into a square about an inch thick. Cut the dough into 12 strips and each strip into two parts. Form a "rope" from each piece by rolling on the board. The "rope" should be about 1/2 inch in diameter. Form a ring and pinch the ends together securely. Try to keep the rings uniform in size and shape. As each is finished place it on the lightly floured board. When you have formed all 24 rings, cover them with a towel and place the board in a warm place for 20 minutes to let the dough rise again.

While the second rising is going on, put at least 4 quarts of water in a big pot and bring it to a boil. Add 1 tbsp sugar. When bagels have risen for 20 minutes, add them to the boiling water, one at a time. You can cook 4 or 5 at once depending on the size of your pot. The bagels will sink to the bottom and then come to the top. Keep the water just at the boiling point and cook for 7 minutes then carefully remove each bagel from the water and place it on a lightly oiled cookie sheet.

When all bagels have been pre-cooked, place the cookie sheet in the oven and cook at 400 degrees until crisp and golden brown, about 25 minutes.

Individual Baked Alaskas

These are easy-to-fix, and sure-to-impress... not a bad combination. Because you use a sponge cake base, they are also a fairly light dessert. Vary the flavor of the ice cream for variety... if you feel like enhancing things even more, try forming a small ball of one flavor of ice cream and encasing it in another flavor.

Yield: 4 servings
Oven setting: 400 degrees Fahrenheit

  3 egg whites
  6 tbsp sugar
  1/8 tsp cream of tartar
  4 commercially prepared shortcake/dessert cups
      (sponge cakes)
  1 pint ice cream

Prepare the baking sheet. If you have a wooden cutting board, cover it with brown wrapping paper and place it on a cookie sheet. If you don't have a wooden cutting board, put three layers of brown wrapping paper on your cookie sheet.

Make a meringue by beating the egg whites until very frothy and then slowly adding the sugar, one tablespoonful at a time. Add the cream of tartar when you have added about half of the sugar. Continue to beat until the egg whites are stiff and hold a peak when the beater is removed.

Arrange the sponge cake cups on the brown wrapping paper and put a scoop of ice cream in each cup. Generously cover all of the ice cream and the cake with the meringue. As you put on the last bit, swirl the spoon slightly so that you have a pretty twist of meringue at the top.

Place in oven and bake for 5 minutes, meringue will be golden. Serve immediately to your admiring guests.

Baking Mix

This is probably the most useful and most versatile mix a cook can have on hand. You can buy it, of course, but it is so easy and inexpensive to make that it seems a natural do-it-yourself. If you would like to have more whole grain in your diet, it works quite well to use half white and half whole wheat flour.

You can use this mix to make biscuits, dumplings, muffins, coffee cake, pancakes and waffles. It can also be used it as an ingredient in casseroles and desserts.

Yield: 12 cups of mix

> **8 cups all-purpose flour** (or 4 cups each all-purpose flour
>   and whole wheat flour)
> **2 tbsp baking powder**
> **1 tbsp salt**
> **2 tsp cream of tartar**
> **1 tsp baking soda**
> **2 cups dry nonfat milk**
> **2 cups shortening**

Mix all dry ingredients together in large bowl (if you have a large mixer it is ideal to use for blending this mix but it can also be done quite adequately using a pastry blender to cut in shortening). Add shortening about a half cup at a time mixing well after each addition. Mixture will be mealy when mixed adequately. Put in air-tight container and store either in refrigerator or at room temperature. Use within about 3 months. Makes about 12 cups of mix.

For Biscuits:
Mix 2 cups of Baking Mix with 1/2 cup water. Bake at 450 for 8-10 minutes.

For Muffins:
Mix 2 cups of Baking Mix with 2 tbsp sugar, 1 beaten egg and 2/3 cup milk. Bake at 400 for 15 minutes.

For Pancakes:
Mix 2 cups of Baking Mix with 1 beaten egg and 1 1/3 cup milk.

For Waffles:
Mix 2 cups of Baking Mix with 1 beaten egg, 2 tbsp oil, and 1 1/3 cup milk.

Banana Daiquiri Sherbet

Often after serving a dinner, you would like a little light dessert... not too sweet, not too heavy, but something to end the meal on a pleasant note. This sherbet is ideal to fill that role. It is refreshing, lightly sweet, and lightly alcoholic.

Yield: Makes 1 quart

   1/2 cup sugar
   1/2 cup water
   1/2 cup light rum
   3 very ripe medium-sized bananas
   1/2 cup lime juice
   1 egg white, lightly beaten

In a small pan, combine the sugar and water and bring to a boil. Boil for 5 minutes, stirring to dissolve the sugar. Remove from the heat and add the rum. Chill until quite cold.

Peel the bananas and cut them into chunks and mix with the lime juice. Puree the bananas and lime juice either in your blender or food processor until very smooth. (You should have about 2 cups of puree.)

Mix with the chilled rum mixture and lightly beaten egg white. At this point you need to freeze the mixture. This is an ideal recipe for using a non-electric ice cream maker that you chill in your freezer or freezer section (such as a *Donvier*). It can also be made in a conventional ice cream maker. It is possible to make in ice trays but you have to stir the mixture frequently as it freezes so that the texture will be as smooth as possible and not simply frozen solid.

Serve garnished with banana slices, or lime slices, or fresh mint, or all three if you like.

Holiday Banana Bread

This is a personal favorite recipe, wonderful for people who just don't like fruitcake. You'll find it to be a pretty addition to a holiday buffet although it's really too good to keep just for the holidays. This makes a nice gift loaf too.

Yield: 1 loaf (about 12 servings)
Oven setting: 350 degrees Fahrenheit

- **1 3/4 cup cake flour** (or all-purpose flour)
- **2/3 cup sugar**
- **3 tsp baking powder**
- **1/2 tsp salt**
- **1/4 tsp baking soda**
- **1/3 cup butter/margarine**
- **2 eggs**
- **1 cup mashed very ripe bananas** (2-3 bananas)
- **1/2 cup chopped walnuts**
- **1 cup diced candied fruit**
- **1/4 cup golden raisins**

Prepare a 9x5-inch loaf pan by greasing and then dusting with flour.

Combine flour, sugar, baking powder, salt and baking soda in a large bowl and mix in the butter/margarine using a pastry blender (or food processor or electric mixer) until it is crumbly and resembles cornmeal.

Beat the eggs lightly and mix in the mashed bananas. Add this mixture to the flour and other dry ingredients. Beat for two minutes to blend thoroughly. Fold in the nuts, diced candied fruit and raisins. Turn the batter into your prepared pan and bake at 350 degrees for between 1 and 1 1/4 hours. Check after 1 hour using a cake tester or wooden pick in the center of the loaf. If it comes out clean, the bread is done. Cool in the pan for 10 minutes and then turn out onto a rack to finish cooling. Allow to cool completely before slicing.

Banana Jam

Bananas are not commonly thought of as a fruit for jam. This is probably because most jams traditionally have been made of fruits that are seasonal and making jams was a way the only-occasionally-available fruits could be enjoyed all year round in earlier times. Nevertheless, flavorful bananas make a good jam. And if you thought peanut butter-and-grape jelly was good, wait till you try peanut butter-and-banana jam!

Yield: About 8 half-pint jars

12 cups sliced ripe bananas (about 6 pounds)
3 cups sugar
1 cup pineapple juice
3/4 cup lemon juice

(See "Canning Using a Boiling Water Bath Process" on page 29 for complete information on how to process the Banana Jam for long-term storage.)

Peel bananas and remove any bruised portions. Cut into slices about 1/4 inch thick. In a large pan combine all ingredients, bring to boil stirring constantly and continue to maintain full rolling boil for 10 minutes while you continue to stir. Reduce heat to medium-low setting and simmer, stirring frequently to keep jam from sticking, for about 20 minutes or until thickened.

Remove from heat and immediately ladle into sterilized half pint jars. Process for 15 minutes in a boiling water bath. (See page 29.) This jam can also be frozen.

Batter to Use for Deep Frying Foods

The problem with most batters suggested for coating fish or vegetables that are to be deep fried is that the batter doesn't stick to the food. This batter will. It is particularly good for coating the fish for Fish and Chips. It also makes great deep fried onion rings and zucchini spears.

Yield: Enough for about 2 pounds of fish or vegetables.

1 cup all-purpose flour
1 tsp baking powder
1/2 cup cornstarch
1 cup water
2 tsp salt
1 tsp sugar
1 tsp oil

Mix all of the ingredients together and blend until there are no lumps.

Preheat the oil in your deep fat fryer to the proper temperature for the food you are cooking.

Dry the fish or the vegetables with a paper towel and dip into the batter. Place in the hot oil one piece at a time. Try to keep the pieces from colliding until the batter has had a chance to set (which it does almost instantly).

Cook until the batter has turned a golden brown, remove to a paper towel to drain and serve at once.

This is very good to use for zucchini, broccoli, peppers, green beans, onion rings and any other firm vegetable.

Beef and Kidney Pie

The English love this dish, in London you'll find it served everywhere from the traditional elegance of Simpson's-in-the-Strand to neighborhood pubs like The Zetland in South Kensington. Like olives, it is something of an acquired taste, but you'll find this recipe is a good way to give it a try... you may be surprised how quickly the "taste for it" is developed! Incidentally, this freezes well so if you cook for fewer than 6, make up two smaller casseroles and freeze the extra for later.

Yield: 6 generous servings
Oven setting: 350 degrees Fahrenheit

For the filling:

    3 pounds round steak about 3/4 inch thick
    1/4 cup flour
    1/4 cup butter/margarine
    3 veal kidneys
    1/2 cup finely chopped onion
    2 cups coarsely chopped mushrooms
    1/2 cup sherry
    1/2 cup red wine
    1 cup beef stock
    2 bay leaves (leave whole)
    1/2 tsp mace
    1/2 tsp dried thyme
    1/4 cup chopped parsley
    1 1/2 tsp Worcestershire sauce
    1 tsp salt
    1/2 tsp finely ground pepper

For the crust:

    1 cup flour
    1/4 tsp salt
    1/3 cup shortening
    1 to 2 tbsp ice water
    1 egg yolk combined with 2 tbsp water

Trim the fat from the round steak and cut it into cubes. Put the flour in a plastic bag and add the meat. Twist the top of the bag to seal and shake it up so that the pieces of meat are covered with flour.

Melt 2 tbsp butter/margarine in a heavy skillet and add the meat. Brown it well on all sides and transfer to the casserole you are going to use for the pie.

Trim the kidneys by removing visible fat, membrane, and the white "core". Cut the kidneys into 1-inch cubes. (If you find the flavor of the kidneys too strong, cover the cubes with milk and allow them to marinate in the milk for an hour. Discard the milk and proceed with the recipe.) Melt the remaining 2 tbsp of butter/margarine in the skillet and add the kidneys. Lightly saute the kidney pieces for a minute or two and then add them to the beef cubes in the casserole.

Saute onions in the skillet until they begin to soften and then add the chopped mushrooms. Continue to saute until onions are transparent then add the sherry, red wine, beef stock, bay leaf, mace, thyme, parsley, Worcestershire sauce, salt and pepper. Cook until bubbles begin to appear around the edge of the pan but don't boil. Pour the sauce over the beef and kidney cubes. Cover and bake at 350 for 1 hour. Remove the casserole from the oven and cool slightly.

While it cools, make the crust: Combine salt and flour in a medium sized bowl. Cut the shortening in using a pastry blender, or use your fingers. Add 1 tbsp ice water and blend. Add additional ice water until the dough will stick together, but be careful to add only what you need because too much water will make the dough tough.

Roll out in an appropriate shape to fit the top of your casserole. Fold in half and make 3 or 4 angled cuts in the dough. Lift the folded dough to the top of the casserole and put it in place. The beef-kidney mixture should be cool enough that you are able to do this without burning your hands. Brush the egg yolk-water mixture over the crust and return the casserole to the oven to bake (at 350) until the crust is brown.

Beer Bread

This is a bread that has a slightly sweet yet tangy flavor that results from the combination of the sugar and the beer. Something of a "guess-what's-in-it" conversation piece for people who have not heard about it. Beer Bread doesn't keep particularly well so plan on using it within a day or two after baking. Leftovers makes nice toast.

Yield: 1 loaf
Oven setting: 375 degrees Fahrenheit

2 cups all purpose self-rising flour
3 tbsp sugar
1 12-ounce can of beer
Melted butter/margarine

You must use self-rising flour for this recipe.

Mix the self-rising flour and sugar together. Stir in beer gently and mix until just blended (don't over mix). Pour into a well-greased 9x5-inch loaf pan. (The dough will look a little lumpy.) Bake 20-25 minutes or until a cake tester comes out clean when pushed into center of loaf. Remove from oven and drizzle with melted butter/margarine. Cool in pan for 5 minutes then turn out onto cooling rack. Can be cut and served warm.

Beer-Cheese Spread

This is a popular spread to keep on hand, good with crackers and also excellent used as a spread on chunks of celery. It also makes a nice home-made gift.

Yield: About 1 1/2 cup cheese spread

1/2 cup mild cheddar cheese
2 hard cooked egg yolks
1 3-ounce pkg of cream cheese
3 anchovies
1/4 cup butter/margarine
1/2 cup warm beer

Bring cheeses and butter/margarine to room temperature. Mash the anchovies and egg yolks together. Grate the cheddar and mix with cream cheese and butter/margarine, then mix in anchovy-egg mixture alternatively with beer. If mixture is too stiff to be spread easily, add a little more beer. Pack mixture into a serving container (a beer mug is a possibility) and serve at room temperature. Store in the refrigerator and use within 3 weeks.

Pickled Beets and Eggs

This special dish comes from those masters of the bountiful table, the Pennsylvania Dutch. It must be made two or three days ahead of the day you plan to serve it, but makes a colorful and unusual addition to a buffet table. You can also slice the eggs and use them with the beet slices to top a bed of mixed greens for an attractive salad.

Yield: 8 servings

4 cups sliced beets, cooked or canned
8 hard-cooked eggs
1 cup sugar
1/2 cup liquid from beets
1/2 cup white vinegar
1 tbsp salt
1/4 tsp pepper
2 dried bay leaves
1 tsp whole cloves

Remove the shells from the hard-cooked eggs. Place them in a large bowl and add the sliced beets.

In a saucepan, combine the sugar, beet liquid, vinegar, salt, pepper, bay leaves, and cloves. Bring to a boil, reduce heat, and simmer for 5 minutes. Put the hot liquid over the sliced beets and whole eggs. Cover the bowl and refrigerate. Gently stir the mixture occasionally so that the eggs color evenly. Marinate the eggs and beet slices in the refrigerator for two days before serving.

Blonde Brownies

There are a lot of people that either don't like or are allergic to chocolate. These bar cookies are of the same consistency and texture as their chocolate cousins, but are made without chocolate... hence "Blonde" Brownies.

Yield: 16 2-inch square brownies
Oven setting: 350 degrees Fahrenheit

For the brownies:

1/4 cup butter/margarine
1 cup brown sugar, firmly packed
1 egg
3/4 cup cake flour
1 tsp baking powder
1/2 tsp salt
1 tsp vanilla extract
1/4 cup unsweetened shredded coconut
1/2 cup chopped nuts (walnuts or pecans are good)

For the frosting:

1/4 cup butter/margarine
1/4 cup brown sugar, firmly packed
2 tbsp milk
1/2 tsp vanilla extract
1 cup powdered sugar

To make Brownies:

Cream 1/4 cup butter/margarine and 1 cup brown sugar until creamy and well blended. Beat egg slightly and add to creamed butter/margarine and sugar mixture. Beat well. Combine flour, baking powder and salt and add to creamed mixture. Mix well. Stir in vanilla, coconut and chopped nuts. Spread batter in a buttered and floured 8-inch square pan. Bake for 25-30 minutes. Cool. Spread with frosting and cut into squares.

To make Frosting:

Melt 1/4 cup butter/margarine in small pan over medium heat. Add 1/4 cup brown sugar, reduce heat and cook for about 3 minutes. Remove from heat and stir in milk. Cool to lukewarm and add vanilla extract. Stir in powdered sugar until spreading consistency is reached.

Portuguese Sweet Bread

This version of the recipe comes from Hawaii where it was introduced by Portuguese sailors in the early days. A similar bread is also found in parts of New England. It is delicious and makes very generous loaves. Good either fresh or toasted. This bread takes several hours to make so be sure to allow yourself plenty of time.

Yield: 3 round loaves
Oven setting: 350 degrees Fahrenheit

- **2 pkgs dry yeast**
- **1/2 cup warm water** (about 100 degrees Fahrenheit)
- **1 cup milk**
- **1/2 cup butter** (butter is much better than margarine in this recipe, but margarine can be used if you wish)
- **2 tsp salt**
- **6 eggs**
- **1 1/2 cups sugar**
- **8-9 cups bread flour** (all-purpose flour can be used if necessary)

Warm a small bowl by rinsing it in hot water. Combine the dry yeast and the warm water in the bowl and gently mix to dissolve the yeast. Set aside.

Warm the milk until bubbles appear around the edges of the pan then remove from heat and add the butter and salt. Allow this mixture to cool to luke warm (until you can comfortably hold the pan on the palm of your hand).

In a large bowl, beat the eggs with the sugar until you have a light, frothy mixture. Add the cooled milk to the eggs, then mix in the yeast. Gradually beat in 3 cups of flour, stir until well mixed. Mix in enough additional flour so that as you stir the dough leaves the sides of the bowl.

At this point, turn the dough out onto a lightly floured board and knead it, adding flour as you go. The dough should not be sticky, but should be smooth and elastic. This will take about 10 minutes. Put the kneaded dough into a large bowl and cover with plastic wrap. Put it in a warm place and allow it to rise until doubled (about 1 1/2 to 2 hours).

Punch the raised dough down and allow it to rest for 10 minutes, lightly covered with a towel. Divide the dough into three parts, and shape each third into a ball. Oil three 8- or 9-inch round cake pans and place one ball in each pan. Flatten the ball to fit the pan and allow the loaves to rise again in a warm place until doubled (it should take about an hour this time.)

Bake in 350 oven for 30 minutes or until golden brown. Remove from oven and brush with melted butter while the loaves are still hot. Cool completely before slicing. (This bread freezes well too.)

Broccoli Parmesan

Here is a super-simple recipe, but one that will be enjoyed by anyone who likes broccoli... and even by some who would normally just as soon have something else. It makes a nice vegetable to serve with an Italian pasta main dish.

Yield: Serves 6

About 6 large stalks of broccoli
1/4 cup finely chopped onion
1/4 cup finely chopped red bell pepper
1 cup bread crumbs made from fresh bread
1/4 cup olive oil
1/4 cup Parmesan cheese (fresh grated if possible)

Remove the thick stems from the broccoli. (You can keep the stems to peel, cut into slivers, and perhaps use in a vegetable stir-fry for another meal.) Cut larger flower heads into easy-to-eat sized pieces. (You should have about 6 or 7 cups of florets.) Steam, cook in microwave (or boil in water if you must but a lot of flavor is lost in the cooking water) until tender.

Warm the olive oil in a skillet and add chopped onions and red peppers. Cook until tender and then add soft bread crumbs and cook until crumbs are golden. Remove from heat and mix in the Parmesan cheese.

To serve, toss the cooked broccoli with the crumb mixture until nicely mixed together.

Biloxi Butter

Biloxi, Mississippi is on the Gulf of Mexico with access to plenty of shrimp. This resource is showcased in this tasty appetizer spread. It is especially good on very crisp melba toast crackers.

Yield: 1 1/2 cups spread

1/2 pound small fresh shrimp, cooked (or 2 cans of small shrimp)
3 tbsp lemon juice
1/2 cup butter/margarine
2 tsp horseradish
1/4 tsp salt
1/4 tsp nutmeg
Liquid pepper sauce to taste (about 1/8 tsp to start, more if you like)

Bring butter/margarine to room temperature. Drain shrimp and put in blender with lemon juice. Add butter/margarine, horseradish, salt, nutmeg and liquid pepper and blend well at slow speed. Press into a mold and chill. Serve with melba toast or other bland dry cracker as an appetizer spread.

Other Seasoned Butters

Seasoned butters are very useful things to have on hand, simple to make but very versatile. You can use the same seasonings with margarine if you prefer. Use the amount of seasoning indicated to flavor 1/2 cup of soft butter or margarine and mix well.

Basil Butter: Add 1/2 tsp dried or 1 1/2 tsp fresh basil. Use on crackers, pasta, chicken breasts, tomatoes or zucchini.

Green Dill: Add 1/4 tsp dried or 1 tsp fresh dill. Use on crackers, chicken breasts, poached eggs, poached salmon, cabbage, carrots, green beans, or zucchini.

Parsley: Add 1 tsp dried or 2 tsp fresh parsley. Use on crackers, pasta, beef steaks, lamp chops, chicken, shellfish, carrots, corn, peas, or potatoes.

Cinnamon: Add 1/2 tsp and 2 tsp sugar. Use on toast, muffins, biscuits, pork chops, acorn squash.

Nutmeg: Add 1/4 tsp Use on pancakes, muffins, chicken breasts, beets, cauliflower or green beans.

Candied Flowers and Leaves

Making candied flowers and leaves to decorate a special cake or dessert takes more patience and time than anything else. It also takes some practice so it is best to try it out once or twice before the day you plan on using candied violets to decorate a cake. The result is worth the effort though. The flowers suggested, by the way, are all edible.

Yield: Depends on size and number of blossoms
Suitable flowers, flower petals, or leaves: violets, rose petals, lilac florets, orange blossoms, mint leaves. Do not use flowers from planting areas where an insecticide has been used.

3 tbsp gum acacia powder (available at pharmacies)
1 cup water
1 cup sugar
food coloring to match blossom colors (optional)
super-fine sugar*
florist wire, toothpicks, paper towels, plastic foam blocks

Work with about fifteen or twenty blossoms or leaves at a time. Gently rinse in cool water and trim so that each has only about 1/4 inch of stem left attached. Attach a piece of florist wire to each (about 3-inch piece). Let dry on paper towel.

In the top of a double boiler over gently boiling water, mix the gum acacia powder in 1/2 cup of the water. Heat, stirring gently, until powder is completely dissolved. Cool to room temperature.

While holding by wire, Dip each blossom or mint leaf individually into cooled gum acacia solution, coating well on all sides. Use a toothpick to separate and shape the blossoms if necessary. Stick wires into foam block so that they do not touch each other. Set aside to dry for at least two hours.

While flowers are drying prepare syrup by combining sugar and remaining 1/2 cup water and cooking without stirring until syrup reaches soft ball stage (238 degrees Fahrenheit on candy thermometer). If food color is to be added, do it at this point. Set syrup aside to cool.

Holding by the wire, individually dip each flower or leaf into cooled syrup and coat all surfaces. Drain off excess then dip in super-fine sugar*. Stick wires into foam blocks and allow to dry thoroughly (at least 8 hours or overnight). Remove wires. If the candied flowers are not to be used immediately, they can be stored by placing them in layers in air tight containers on sheets of waxed paper (do not use aluminum foil or plastic wrap).

*You can make your own super-fine sugar by putting regular granulated sugar in your blender and turning it on and off a few times.

Canning Using a Boiling Water Bath Process

A "boiling water bath" can be use to process all fruits, jams, preserves, conserves, chutneys, and most condiments for long-term storage. It cannot be used in canning vegetables, meat dishes, or combination dishes such as chili. For those things, you must use a pressure cooker so that the internal temperature of the food in the bottles can be raised sufficiently.

Home canning is fun and satisfying. It is not complicated and, if you follow a few simple steps, you can be assured of fruit and other things you will be proud to serve and say "I canned it myself."

You will need:

Large boiling water bath canner with rack and lid
Glass canning bottles (use only canning bottles made by commercial manufacturers, recycled bottles that have contained products you have purchased are not made of a glass that is tempered to resist temperature changes and they are easily broken in the canner which makes a terrific mess)
Metal rings (if you are recycling rings you have used before, check to make sure they are not rusted)
New metal bottle lids

Getting ready:

Fill the canner with enough water to come to about 1 inch over the tops of the bottles and bring to a boil.

While the canning water is heating, wash the bottles in your dishwasher (or by hand in very hot water). Leave in the dishwasher until needed.

Separate the lids and put them in a pan of boiling water to sterilize.

Fill and process the bottles:

Fill the bottles with whatever it is your are going to can. Leave about 1/2 inch of space at the top of the bottle because the hot product is going to expand a little. If you don't leave some space for expansion, the liquid will force its way out of the bottle under the lid and the seal will be lost.

With a wet paper towel carefully wipe the top of each jar. Any food or liquid left there could prevent the lid from sealing.

Place a sterilized lid on each bottle. Put on a metal ring and tighten it down. Place the bottles in the canner.

Start timing the processing from the time the water comes to a boil again. Timing varies depending on what you are processing so check individual recipes.

If you live at an altitude well above sea level, you should add 1 minute of processing time for each 1000 feet above sea level to compensate for the slightly lower temperature at which water boils. (For a dense filling, like Apple Pie Filling, add 2 minutes extra for each 1000 feet in altitude.)

When processing is completed, use bottle tongs to remove each bottle from the hot water and place it on a cooling rack in a place that is protected from drafts. It is best not to let the bottles touch each other during cooling.

Store the finished product:

When completely cooled, check the seal on each lid by pressing down. If the lid is firmly in place, the bottle is ready for storage in a coolish, dry place.

If the lid "gives" when you press it, a seal has not been made. In that case you can either put the food in the refrigerator and treat it as though it were cooked but not preserved, or you can put it in a container and freeze. Sometimes you hear that you can re-process the bottle again, but that isn't a good idea because the produce is cooked each time it is processed and re-processing tends to make food mushy and unattractive.

Try to use canned foods within about a year. After that time they are safe to eat but begin to lose flavor.

Never use food from a bottle that has lost its seal (the lid is not firmly in place), or food that shows sign of molding. Sometimes people will say that it is alright to eat jams that have mold on top... not so. The mold tendrils extend throughout the bottle even if they are only visible on top. Just throw any molded food away immediately.

Caramel Sauce

Sometimes one would just like to forget about calories altogether. This is a sauce for those times. Maybe you would prefer to indulge in a rich fudge sauce, but for caramel sauce fanciers, nothing can equal a caramel sundae.

Yield: About 2 cups sauce

> **3 cups brown sugar, loosely packed**
> **3 tbsp flour (or 3 tsp powdered arrowroot)**
> **1/2 cup butter/margarine, melted**
> **1 1/2 cup boiling water**
> **2 tsp vanilla extract**
> **1/2 cup chopped nuts if you like**

Mix brown sugar and flour (or arrowroot) together in the top of a double boiler. (Arrowroot will make a less "pasty" sauce. If you use arrowroot, however, don't let the sauce boil or it will not thicken properly.) Add melted butter/margarine and stir well. Over gently boiling water, cook stirring occasionally for five minutes.

Slowly add boiling water to the sugar mixture while continuing to stir constantly. Continue to cook and stir until sauce is thickened. Remove from heat and stir in vanilla extract.

You can use artificial vanilla flavoring if you wish, but true vanilla (although expensive) makes a noticeable difference in the results. See Flavored Extracts recipe for a simple way to make your own vanilla extract at minimal cost.

Serve immediately or cool and store in refrigerator up to about 3 months.

Scandinavian Cardamom Rolls

These fragrant rolls are perfect to serve for brunch or a special lunch. Although they are, of course, very best when they are fresh from the oven, they can also be made a day in advance and stored in an air-tight plastic bag. They freeze quite well and can be quickly thawed for breakfast.

Yield: 18 rolls
Oven setting: 375 degrees Fahrenheit

> **1 pkg dry yeast** (1 scant tbsp)
> **1/2 warm water** (90-100 degrees Fahrenheit)
> **2 cups milk**
> **1/2 cup butter/margarine**
> **1 tsp whole cardamom seeds***
> **2 eggs**
> **1 tsp salt**
> **1/2 cup sugar**
> **7 cups bread flour** (all-purpose can be used)
> **Melted butter/margarine**

*Whole cardamom seeds are the small seeds inside the tan colored cardamom pods. To get at the seeds, just break open the pods.

Dissolve the yeast in the warm water. Set aside for 5 minutes.

Heat the milk until bubbles appear around the edge of the pan. Cut the butter/margarine into pieces and add to the milk. Stir until the butter/margarine has melted. Set aside to cool to lukewarm.

Crush the cardamom seeds in your blender or in a mortar and pestle until they are coarsely ground.

Combine milk-butter mixture, yeast, cardamom, eggs, salt and sugar in a bowl and mix well. Add flour 1 cup at a time until the batter will not easily absorb any more and then turn out onto a floured board and knead in the remaining flour. Continue kneading for about 10 minutes until dough is smooth and elastic. (This can also be done with the dough hook of a heavy-duty electric mixer or in a food processor. Follow manufacturer's directions.)

Turn the dough into a large oiled bowl. Turn the dough over so that the oiled side is up and allow to raise in a warm place until it is doubled in size (about an hour).

Punch the dough down and divide it into two parts. Let the dough rest for 10 minutes while you prepare baking pans.

Use butter/margarine to grease two square cake pans (8- or 9-inch pans). Form nine balls out of each half of the dough and arrange the balls in 3 rows of 3 in each pan. Cover and allow to raise until doubled in size (about a half hour). Gently brush the tops of the rolls with milk.

Bake at 375 degrees for about 25-30 minutes or until golden brown. Serve immediately or cool and store in air-tight bags in the refrigerator and use within a week.

Catsup

Once you have made this delightful concoction, you will never go back to commercially-prepared catsup again if you can help it. Incidentally, although "catsup" tends to be thought of as a tomato-based condiment, in earlier times catsups (or ketchups as the sauces were sometimes called), were made from such diverse ingredients as walnuts, grapes, mushrooms, and berries.

The aroma in the kitchen while this recipe for catsup is cooking is a treat in itself.

Yield: About 8 pints
Oven setting: if cooked in oven, 300 degrees Fahrenheit

   10 pounds very ripe tomatoes*
   3 sweet red peppers
   3 green peppers
   5 medium-large onions
   4 cups cider vinegar
   2 cups white sugar
   3 tbsp salt (add more to taste)
   2 cups brown sugar
   2 tsp ground allspice
   3 tsp ground cinnamon
   1 tsp ground cloves
   5 tsp dry ground mustard
   (Liquid pepper sauce to taste if you like a "hot" catsup)

*Check with your County Extension Agent for local varieties that are suitable for this purpose.

(See "Canning Using a Boiling Water Process" on page 29 for complete information on how to process catsup for long-term storage.)

Wash the tomatoes. Remove core, skin, and seeds (in that order) and coarsely chop. Wash, remove seeds, and coarsely chop the peppers. Chop the onions. Mix all of the vegetables together. Put 1 cup of vinegar in your blender or food processor, add some of the vegetable mixture and puree. Continue to add vinegar and vegetables until all have been processed.

Combine the dry ingredients in a small bowl.

Oven cooking:

Pour vegetable puree into a roasting pan and mix in the dry ingredients. (Add liquid pepper sauce if you are going to use it.) Bake uncovered at

300 stirring occasionally until it has reduced itself by half. This will take 4-5 hours depending on how much juice the tomatoes contained.

Stove-top cooking:

Catsup can also be cooked to the desired thickness on top of the stove in a large heavy kettle. Stir often if cooked on top of the stove because the catsup can easily stick and the resulting scorched taste can spoil the entire batch. Use a heavy kettle for stove-top cooking because light weight aluminum tends to have "hot spots" that will encourage sticking.

When reduced to the desired thickness, Pour into sterilized jars and process in boiling water bath for 15 minutes. (See page 29.)

The catsup is best if you allow it to mellow for about a week before you serve it the first time.

Golden Champagne Punch

This is a delightfully light and fresh tasting punch that is good for summer celebrations. It is also a nice choice for weddings any time. One pretty way to garnish and keep the punch cool is to float in the punch bowl an ice ring frozen with flowers (see page 92 for directions).

Yield: 8-10 servings (about 3 1/2 quarts)

> 1 6-ounce can orange juice concentrate
> 1 cup lemon juice
> 2 1/2 cups pineapple juice
> 1 cup granulated sugar
> 1 fifth sauterne wine
> 2 fifths champagne
> Large block of ice
> Sliced oranges or limes, or whole strawberries

Mix juices and sugar and stir until sugar is dissolved. Cover and chill for at least 4 hours. Chill the sauterne and champagne.

To serve, pour the juice mixture over the block of ice in a punch bowl and add sauterne and champagne. Stir together lightly. Garnish with fruit if you like.

Cheese and Cauliflower Loaf

Here is a vegetable dish that is simple to make, looks nice on a plate and is something a little different. Cauliflower, although "good for us", is not one of the world's most popular vegetables. This casserole, however, mellows the taste of the cauliflower and the cheese adds its own sharp flavor.

Yield: Serves 4
Oven setting: 450 degrees Fahrenheit

  1 large cauliflower
  2 eggs
  2/3 cup milk
  Salt and pepper
  3 tbsp butter/margarine
  1/2 cup Parmesan, freshly grated if possible (you can
      substitute Romano cheese if you prefer it)

Clean the cauliflower and break the head into pieces. Cook until just tender then place in cold water to cool quickly. In your food processor or blender, make a coarse puree out of the cooked cauliflower. (Don't let the puree become too smooth, you want to have some texture to the final dish.)

In a large bowl beat the eggs slightly and add the milk and salt and pepper to taste. Add the cauliflower and mix well.

Use 1 tbsp of the butter/margarine to grease a 8x8-inch baking dish and pour in the mixture. Cut the rest of the butter/margarine into small pieces and distribute on the top. Top with the grated Parmesan cheese. Bake at 450 degrees for 20 minutes or until the top is golden brown.

Cheese Rounds

These are a simple appetizer that you can keep on hand in the freezer to bake as you need. By varying the garnish that you roll the dough in you can make some colorful treats. These little wafers are good not only as an appetizer but also to serve with salads.

Yield: About 24 appetizers

1 jar of process cheese spread (savory flavor, not sweet)
1/2 cup baking mix
(Sesame seeds, dried parsley, paprika, or poppy seeds)

Mix cheese and baking mix. Shape into a roll about 1 inch in diameter. Roll in: sesame seeds, or dried parsley, or poppy seeds.

Chill for at least 2 hrs. Cut into 1/4 inch slices (turn the roll as you cut slices to keep them round). Bake at 375 for about 10 minutes. Best when served warm, but can be baked in advance if necessary.

Preparing Chicken Breasts

Chicken breasts are among the most versatile meats to cook. Because they do not have a strong flavor of their own, they lend themselves well to all kinds of sauces and methods of cooking. They are also not expensive and certainly agreeable to serve to guests as well as family. The final bonus is that they are not loaded with fat and so are a real benefit for those who must watch fat intake or are concerned about cholesterol.

Here is an efficient and cost-effective way to prepare them.

Your best value is to buy whole chickens. There are several reasons for this. Most importantly, you get to have the whole chicken to use... the breasts in one dish, the other meat in another, the wings set aside for something else, and the bones into the stock pot to make that cooking essential, chicken stock.

First, skin the chicken:

With a sharp knife, remove each wing at the shoulder. Cut the end portion of the wing off (and put it with bones for the stock pot). Then cut the remaining wing into two portions at the joint. Accumulate these wing sections in a sealable bag in your freezer until you have enough to make a meal or use for appetizers.

Using the sharpest knife you have, cut through the skin in a straight line down the backbone and then from top to bottom in the front as well. Put the knife down and hook one of your index fingers though the "ring" where the shoulder is. With your other hand, pull the skin straight down, clear off over the end of the leg. Either discard the skin or add it to the stock pot. Cut all of the excess fat away. (When you see where it accumulates on the chicken you can see what comes from sitting around in a hen house all day doing nothing but eating!)

Second, separate the parts to use:

Cut the thigh away from the body at the hip bone. (The thigh and leg will be used in another dish. They can also be cooked in advance and used in chicken sandwiches or dishes calling for cooked chicken.)

Next remove the breast meat by keeping your knife very close to the ribs and easing the meat away from the bones.

Finally you are left with the body bones which go into the stockpot.

As you can see, one chicken can easily contribute to four different meals this way.

And now here are some ways you can use the breasts...

Cold Chicken Wrapped in Ham

This is a dish that lends itself well to summer buffets or picnics. It can be made early in the day. It's easy to prepare, easy to serve, and easy to eat... all of which are in its favor. If you take it away on a picnic, be sure to keep it cool until you serve. You may wish to wait to add the sour cream sauce after you arrive at your destination.

Yield: 6 servings

> 6 chicken breast halves
> 1/4 cup flour
> 1/2 tsp garlic powder
> 1/2 tsp paprika
> 1/2 tsp chili powder
> 1/2 tsp salt
> 4 tbsp butter/margarine
> 3/4 cup dry white wine (or chicken broth)
> 8 ounces of thin sliced smoked ham (packaged ham works well)
> 1 cup sour cream
> 1 tsp finely grated lemon rind
> 2 tbsp water (or more as needed to thin sour cream to pouring consistency)

(See "Preparing Chicken Breasts" on page 39 for complete information on preparing chicken breasts.)

Cut each half breast crosswise into strips about an inch wide.

Combine the flour, garlic powder, paprika, chili powder and salt. Pour the dry ingredients into a plastic bag and add the pieces of chicken breast a few at a time. Shake well to coat each piece on all sides.

Melt the butter/margarine in a large skillet and saute the chicken pieces until lightly browned.

Add the wine (or chicken broth) to the skillet with the chicken pieces and simmer gently for 15 minutes. Remove the chicken pieces from the liquid and place in refrigerator to chill.Separate the thinly sliced smoked ham into individual pieces. When the chicken has cooled, place a piece of chicken on each piece of ham and fold the ham around the chicken. Arrange with smooth side of meat up on a platter.

Combine the sour cream with lemon rind and water. Pour in a thin stream across the center of the chicken-ham "packages" and serve the remainder of the sauce in a separate small pitcher.

Curried Chicken Breasts

Unlike most chicken curries, this is not pieces of chicken in a thick sauce flavored with curry powder. Rather it is whole chicken breasts baked in quite a thin curry sauce. By all means serve with your favorite pilaf and curry condiments as you would other chicken curries.

Yield: Serves 6
Oven setting: 350 degrees Fahrenheit

- **6 chicken breast halves**
- **1/2 cup all-purpose flour**
- **3 tbsp butter/margarine**
- **1/2 cup finely chopped onion**
- **2 cloves of garlic, finely minced**
- **1-2 tbsp curry powder** (to your preference)
- **1/2 tsp salt**
- **1/2 tsp ground ginger**
- **1/2 tsp ground cinnamon**
- **1/4 tsp ground pepper**
- **2 tbsp lime** (or lemon) **juice**
- **2 cups chicken broth**

See "Preparing Chicken Breasts" on page 39 for complete information on preparing breasts.

Roll each breast piece in flour to coat completely.

Melt the butter/margarine in a large skillet. Add the chicken pieces and brown lightly on all sides. Remove and place in an oven-safe baking dish.

Add the chopped onion and garlic to the butter/margarine remaining in the skillet and cook until onion is golden. Add the curry powder, salt, ginger, cinnamon, and pepper and cook for 2 or 3 minutes while you stir constantly. Add the chicken broth all at once and, using a small whisk, stir into a smooth sauce.

Pour the sauce over the chicken breast pieces, cover and bake at 350 degrees for 1 hour. Carefully pour the sauce off the chicken and into a small saucepan and add the lime or lemon juice. Keep the chicken warm while you bring the sauce to a boil and reduce its volume slightly.

To serve, arrange the chicken on a bed of rice pilaf and pour some of the sauce over it. The rest of the sauce can be served separately. (The sauce can be strained to remove onion and garlic if you like.)

Some condiments that go well with this include: a fruit chutney, chopped peanuts, grated unsweetened coconut, crushed pineapple, plain yogurt, chopped green onions, or a variety of other things.

Chicken Breasts Parmesan

Here is a super dish to serve when you have a few friends in for dinner. It has all the advantages... easy to fix (you can even fix it in stages as you have time), relatively inexpensive, easy to serve, and (best of all) delicious! A good vegetable dish to serve with this is the Broccoli Parmesan on page 26.

Yield: Serves 6

6 chicken breast halves
1/2 cup all-purpose flour
2 eggs
1 cup bread crumbs (dried are best,
    but fresh will do)
1 tsp salt
1/2 tsp onion powder
1/4 tsp garlic powder
1/4 tsp paprika
1/2 cup chopped onions
1-2 crushed cloves of garlic
2 8-ounce cans of tomato sauce
1/2 tsp oregano
1/2 tsp basil
1/4 cup olive oil
2/3 cup Parmesan cheese (fresh grated if possible)
8 ounces mozzarella cheese

(See "Preparing Chicken Breasts" on page 39 for complete information on preparing breasts.)

Using a meat mallet (or some other firm but blunt tool) flatten each chicken breast into an oval shape.

Get out three bowls and put the flour in the first one. Lightly beat the eggs in the second bowl. In the third bowl, combine the bread crumbs with the salt, onion powder, garlic powder and paprika.

Dip the flattened chicken breasts first into the flour, then into the beaten eggs, and finally cover well with the seasoned crumbs. Place each prepared chicken breast on a rack and put them in the refrigerator for at least thirty minutes to let the coating set.

Prepare the Sauce

Make an Italian-seasoned tomato sauce by first lightly sauteing the chopped onion and garlic and then adding the two cans of tomato sauce, the oregano, and basil. Simmer for 20 minutes.

Heat the olive oil in a large skillet and saute the chicken breasts until they are golden brown and then arrange them in a shallow baking dish.

Pour the sauce over the chicken breasts, spreading so they are lightly covered with the sauce. Top with the grated parmesan cheese and bake at 350 for 30 minutes.

Slice the mozzarella cheese into thin slices. Remove the baking dish from the oven and arrange on top of the chicken. Return to the oven for another 10 minutes to melt the mozzarella and serve.

Chicken Breasts with Spiced Cranberry Sauce

This is a simple dish to make, but very complex in flavor. The old stand-by canned jellied cranberry sauces takes on an entirely new personality when the spices and mustard are added.

Yield: Serves 6

6 chicken breast halves
1 8-ounce can of jellied cranberry sauce
1/2 cup sweet sherry
1 1/2 cup chicken stock
1/2 tsp dry mustard
1/4 tsp ground ginger
1/4 tsp ground nutmeg
1/4 tsp Chinese five-spice*
2 tsp prepared sweet mustard*
1 tbsp brown sugar
3 tbsp butter/margarine

(See "Preparing Chicken Breasts" on page 39 for complete information on preparing breasts.)

Flatten the breasts using a mallet or other blunt tool. Don't cut the breast through, however, just hit it hard enough to flatten to about 1/4-1/2 inch.

In a small saucepan combine the jellied cranberry sauce (chop into chunks to speed melting), sweet sherry, chicken stock, dry and prepared mustard, ginger, nutmeg, and Chinese Five-spice*, and brown sugar. Over high heat bring to a boil and then reduce heat and simmer for 10 minutes.

(*If you cannot find Chinese Five-spice, you can make your own by using the recipe for "Chinese Five-Spice" on page 75. If you do not have prepared sweet mustard on hand, add 1/2 honey to the sauce.)

Melt the butter/margarine in a skillet and saute the chicken breasts until lightly browned and cooked through. Remove from the skillet and keep warm while you prepare the sauce.

Add the cranberry sauce mixture to the butter/margarine in the skillet. With the heat on high, reduce the sauce to about half of its original volume and pour it over the chicken breasts to serve.

Chicken with 40 Cloves of Garlic

Don't gasp... that really does say "40"! However, by cooking for a long time, the garlic flavor permeates the chicken and the garlic itself mellows in flavor at the same time. Yes, it certainly tastes like garlic, but it doesn't knock you down. It just lets you know what a nice taste garlic can have when it has been softened by gentle cooking.

Yield: Serves 6-8
Oven setting: 350 degrees Fahrenheit

3 frying chickens cut into serving size pieces
1/4 cup olive oil
2 large carrots
6 stalks of celery
2 large onions
40 cloves of garlic (5 or 6 heads should do)
1/2 cup chopped fresh parsley
1 cup dry white wine
Salt and pepper

If you buy whole chickens, cut them into serving size pieces. Rub the pieces with olive oil.

Peel the carrots and cut into chunks about 2-3 inches long. Cut the celery into pieces about the same length. Cut the onions in half lengthwise (not across as for slices) and divide each half into long narrow pieces (match sticks). Peel the garlic but leave whole.

Arrange the chicken pieces in a casserole with a tight lid. Distribute the carrots, celery, garlic, and parsley over the chicken. Sprinkle with salt and pepper. Pour the dry white wine over all. Put a layer of foil over all, large enough that it will stick out after the lid has been put in place. Put the lid on the casserole and bake at 350 for 1 1/2 hours.

Chili Sauce

Chili Sauce is similar, but not identical, to Mexican salsa. This is an old recipe though, certainly pre-dating our interest in ethnic foods of all kinds. Housewives traditionally made chili sauce and home-made catsup to use up excess tomatoes from the garden at the end of summer. It is spicy rather than hot. See the recipe for Salsa on page 156 as a comparison.

Yield: About 8 pints

    2 1/2 quarts chopped tomatoes (about 8 pounds)*
    2 cups chopped onions
    2 cups chopped green peppers
    1 1/4 cup sugar
    1 tbsp ground cinnamon
    1 tbsp allspice
    1 tbsp cloves
    1 tbsp salt
    1 cup sugar
    1 1/2 cups white vinegar

*Check with your County Extension Agent for local varieties that are suitable for this purpose.

(See "Canning Using a Boiling Water Bath Process" on page 29 for complete information on how to process the Chili Sauce for long-term storage.)

This will take a large kettle and you should use one that is fairly heavy so that the heat will be evenly conducted throughout with no hot spots. Tomatoes have a terrible tendency to "catch" and burn and if that happens, your entire batch can be spoiled.

In the kettle combine all of the ingredients. Bring to a boil over high heat and then immediately reduce the heat to low and simmer until the sauce is thick enough for your taste. This will take from 1 to 3 hours depending on how much juice the tomatoes contained. Stir regularly and often while the sauce is cooking.

When the sauce is thick enough, pour the hot chili sauce into prepared bottles and process in a boiling water bath canner. Chili sauce should be processed for 15 minutes. (See page 29.)

Use this as a topping for hamburgers, on eggs, with cold cuts, in sauces and spreads...

Chili con Queso Dip

Chili con Queso means Chili with Cheese. Strictly speaking, it is probably more Cali-Mex or Tex-Mex than truly Mexican. Whatever its exact origin, it has been popular for a long time. It makes a specially good dip for the ubiquitous tortilla chips.

Yield: About 3 cups

1 cup chopped onion
2 cloves garlic chopped
1/4 cup cooking oil
3-4 cups of canned tomatoes
1 small can chopped green chili peppers
1/4 cup finely chopped fresh green bell pepper
1/4 tsp salt
Pepper to taste
1/2 cup half-and-half cream (light cream)
2 cup sharp cheddar, grated
1 tsp worcestershire sauce

Saute onions in oil until golden, add garlic and cook slightly. Chop canned tomatoes into small pieces and add with canned chili peppers, fresh peppers, salt and pepper. Cook for 5 minutes. Add half-and-half, grated cheddar, and worcestershire sauce and stir until cheese is melted. Keep warm in a container over hot water or on a warming tray and serve hot with crackers, tortilla chips or crudites as a dip.

Crunchy Chocolate Candy

There are several chocolate bars on the market that contain some sort of "crunch" to lighten the chocolate. A home-made version is easy and inexpensive to make. This is a fun project for the whole family, simple enough for the youngest to participate.

Yield: 9x13-inch pan to be cut as you choose

2 cups *Rice Krispies* **or some similar cereal**
1/4 cup butter/margarine
6 ounces semisweet chocolate chips
1/4 cup white corn syrup
1 tsp vanilla
1 1/2 cups sifted powdered sugar

Take some extra butter/margarine and grease a 9x13-inch baking pan. Put the cereal into a plastic bag and mash it slightly so that the pieces are slightly broken but not made into a powder.

Combine the butter/margarine, chocolate chips, and corn syrup in a pan. Place it over low heat and stir continuously until the butter and chocolate are melted and the mixture is blended. Do not overheat while you are doing this. Remove from the heat and add the vanilla. Stir in the powdered sugar (a whisk will help you make it smooth).

Add the crushed cereal and stir in well until everything is mixed together then, working quickly, scoop the mixture into the buttered pan and flatten it and smooth the surface. Chill until firm. Cut into squares or rectangles and wrap if you like.

These will store at room temperature.

Hot Chocolate for Adults Only

Who said that hot chocolate was just for kids... not anyone who tries this elegant hot drink!

Yield: 4 servings

1/2 cup chocolate chips
3 cups milk
1 cup half-and-half (light cream)
1/2 cup sugar
1/2 cup rum
1/2 cup almond or hazelnut flavored liqueur
Whipped cream and cinnamon sticks

Melt chocolate chips over simmering water or in microwave according to manufacturer's directions.

Combine milk, half-and-half and sugar in a saucepan and bring up to simmer (so that bubbles are just beginning to form around the edge of the pan). Very slowly add about 1 cup of the milk mixture to the melted chocolate and mix thoroughly. Pour chocolate mixture back into remaining milk mixture. Stir in rum and liqueur.

Pour into mugs and top with a dollop of whipped cream and a cinnamon stick. Serve at once.

Chocolate Mint Torte

This is very rich so keep the servings small! Those who really can't resist chocolate desserts may be back for seconds...

Yield: 10-12 servings
Oven setting: 350 degrees Fahrenheit

Crust:

> **1 cup chocolate cookie crumbs** (15-17 cookies)
> **2 tbsp melted butter/margarine**

Filling:

> **1/2 cup softened butter/margarine**
> **3/4 cup sugar**
> **3 ounces unsweetened chocolate**
> **1 tsp vanilla extract**
> **1 tsp peppermint extract**
> **3 eggs**
> **1/2 cup whipping cream**
> **Grated unsweetened chocolate**

Mix chocolate cookie crumbs and melted butter/margarine. Press firmly into the bottom of an 8-inch spring-form pan (or use a pie pan if you don't have a spring-form). Bake for 7-8 minutes. Cool.

Use your electric mixer to prepare the filling. Cream butter/margarine until smooth and gradually add the sugar. Melt the chocolate over simmering (not boiling) water in a double boiler or in the microwave according to manufacturer's instructions. Combine melted chocolate, vanilla and peppermint extracts and blend into butter/sugar mixture. Add eggs one at a time and beat about 3 minutes after adding each egg.

Beat cream until it holds a firm peak. Fold whipped cream into chocolate mixture. Gently spread into prepared crust. Sprinkle with grated chocolate (or use chocolate sprinkles). Loosely cover with plastic wrap (try not to let the plastic touch the surface of the torte). Chill for at least 3 hours.

Chocolate Sauce

This is a basic recipe the can be varied to meet your needs of the moment or special preferences. It is a very handy sauce to have on hand and you'll find you don't have to store it long because it will quickly be used up.

Yield: About 1 cup of sauce

2 ounces semi-sweet baking chocolate*
2 tbsp butter/margarine
1/2 cup boiling water
1 1/2 cup sugar
1/8 tsp salt
1 tsp vanilla extract or some other flavoring

Melt chocolate in top of double boiler. Stir in butter/margarine. Add boiling water and mix. Add sugar and salt. Cook, stirring only occasionally, for about 15 minutes. Remove from heat and stir in vanilla extract. Serve immediately or cool and store in a covered container in your refrigerator. Sauce will keep up to 3 months and is best if reheated slightly.

*If you do not have baking chocolate on hand you can substitute 3 tbsp cocoa powder, 2 tsp shortening and 3 tbsp sugar for each ounce of baking chocolate called for in any recipe.

Some flavor variations to use instead of vanilla extract:
1 tsp mint extract
2 tbsp chopped nuts
1 tsp almond extract
1 tsp instant coffee granules
1 tsp orange extract
1 tsp maraschino cherry syrup and 2 tbsp chopped cherries
1 tbsp apricot preserves

Chocolate Truffles

There's no way around it, truffles are time consuming to make. They are not inexpensive to make either. They take a great deal of patience. But the result... well, the result is melt-in-your-mouth wonderfulness. This is a candy that makes a lovely gift, and one or two make a splendid dessert anytime.

Yield: 4 dozen individual truffles

    1/2 cup sugar
    1/2 cup whole almonds
    1 tbsp mild oil (such as corn or sunflower)
    12 ounces semi-sweet chocolate chips
    1/4 cup unsalted butter
    2 tbsp rum or brandy
    1 tbsp grated orange zest
    1/2 cup unsweetened cocoa
    2 tbsp whipping cream

Caramelize the sugar by putting it into a small heavy pan and heating over low heat until it has melted and browned slightly. Add the almonds and continue to cook until the sugar darkens to a medium brown. You have to watch very carefully to make sure the sugar doesn't burn at this point. Pour the hot sugar-almond mixture out onto a well greased tray or cookie sheet and spread to form a thin layer. Cool completely. Break the sheet of sugar and nuts (which can now be called "praline") into pieces and grind to a fine powder in your blender or food processor.

Next melt half the chocolate chips in the top of a double boiler (or in your microwave following manufacturer's directions). Gently stir in the butter, rum or brandy, orange rind, cream and praline powder. Chill for about an hour or until firm. Using your fingers or a melon ball scoop, shape the chocolate mixture into 1/2 inch balls and place in your freezer to chill until very firm.

For the outside coating, melt the remaining chocolate chips and cool to lukewarm. Take the hardened truffles from the freezer and roll each in the melted chocolate. This is perhaps the ultimate in messy jobs, but fun, especially when several people are helping the cook. The coating of chocolate should be thin, just enough to cover the truffle.

As a final touch roll the coated pieces in the powdered cocoa. Store in an air-tight container in the refrigerator (they won't last long). For long term storage, or to make well in advance of a party, place them in a flat container, wrap well with foil and freeze. They are really best when they are eaten within a week and not frozen however.

Chocolate Waffles

*Chocolate waffles and peppermint ice cream are a perfect combina-
tion. Each flavor complements the other and the result is very special. On
the other hand, chocolate waffles are good by themselves or with some
other flavor ice cream too. This is an excellent dish to prepare for an "after"
party... after the game, after the movie, after the concert.*

Yield: 4 Servings

1 egg
2 tbsp butter/margarine
1/3 cup milk
3 tbsp sugar
3 tbsp almond-flavored liqueur (or 1 tsp almond extract)
1/3 cup sour cream
1/4 cup chocolate syrup
2/3 cup all-purposes flour
1 tsp baking powder
1/4 tsp baking soda

Separate the egg and melt the butter/margarine. Mix together the milk,
sugar, sour cream, almond-flavored liqueur or almond extract, chocolate
syrup, melted butter/margarine and egg yolk.

In another bowl mix the dry ingredients together. Beat egg white until
firm but not dry. Stir liquid mixture into dry ingredients until well mixed.
Fold in beaten egg white.

Preheat your waffle iron. When hot, pour batter onto grids and bake until
done.

Cinnamon Pull-apart Breakfast Rolls

Just the aroma of these rolls baking is enough to move the most recalcitrant teenager to the breakfast table. You can make the dough the day before so that all you have to do is shape the rolls and bake for a lovely weekend breakfast treat.

Yield: 1 tube pan of rolls... serves about 6
Oven setting: 375 degrees Fahrenheit

- 1 cup boiling water
- 1/2 cup sugar
- 1/2 cup butter/margarine
- 1 tsp salt
- 1 pkg yeast
- 2 eggs, beaten
- 4 1/2 cups bread flour
- 3/4 cup butter/margarine, melted
- 1 1/2 cups sugar
- 1 tbsp cinnamon

The day before:

Pour boiling water over sugar, butter/margarine and salt and mix until butter/margarine melts. Cool to lukewarm. Dissolve yeast in 1/4 cup warm water and add to mixture. Add beaten eggs. Stir in flour and mix to make a soft dough. Place in a large mixing bowl, cover with plastic wrap and refrigerate overnight.

The next morning:

Preheat oven to 375 degrees F. Remove dough from refrigerator and allow to come up to room temperature (about 30 minutes). Melt 3/4 cup margarine and mix with 1 1/2 cups sugar and cinnamon. Form dough into balls about 1 1/2 inches in diameter and roll each one in the cinnamon-sugar-butter mixture. Place balls into a tube or loaf pan. Bake for about 45-50 minutes or until nicely browned.

Cioppino

Tradition tells us that this delectable soup-stew is a gift to us from Italian immigrants to the coast of Northern California. They based it on traditional fish soups but modified the ingredients to take advantage of the fish on hand.

Whatever its origin, cioppino is a great dish to serve for an informal supper. All you need is cioppino, a big green salad and some crusty French or Italian bread... with or without the garlic butter!

Yield: Serves 6

> 1 **pound fish fillets** (halibut, sea bass, red snapper, or any other firm fish)
> 1 **pound shellfish** (crab, prawns, clams, scallops)
> 3 **onions**
> 1 **green pepper**
> 2 **cloves of garlic**
> 3 **tbsp olive oil**
> 1 **28-ounce can of tomatoes**
> 3 **8-ounce cans of tomato sauce**
> 1 **6-ounce can of tomato paste**
> 2 **cups water**
> 2 **tsp dried basil**
> 1 **tsp dried oregano**
> 1/4 **cup chopped parsley**

Remove any shells from shell fish. Cut fish fillets into bite size pieces. Refrigerate fish. Chop onions, pepper and garlic. Warm olive oil and saute the vegetables until they are tender and lightly browned. Add the canned tomatoes, tomato sauce and paste, water, and spices. Simmer for 1 hour. Add the fish fillet pieces and shellfish and cook an additional 15 minutes. Serve in large bowls garnished with chopped parsley.

Clam Spread

There are a lot of recipes for clam dip or clam spread but most are based on either sour cream or cream cheese. Very good, but also with quite a few calories and also a fair share of cholesterol. For those who would prefer less of both, and as an added benefit proportionally more calcium, here is an alternative.

Yield: About 3/4 cup spread. This amount will serve about 4 as an appetizer or make two substantial sandwiches.

- 1/2 cup small-curd cottage cheese
- 2 tbsp mayonnaise
- 1 tsp lemon juice
- 1/2 tsp worcestershire sauce
- 1/4 tsp garlic powder
- Several drops *Tabasco* Sauce, to taste
- 1 8-ounce can minced or chopped clams

Combine all ingredients except clams in blender or food processor and mix thoroughly until smooth. Pour into bowl and stir in clams. (If possible, make several hours before you plan to serve it so that flavors can blend.) Cover and store in refrigerator. This spread can be used either as an appetizer spread on crackers or thin slices of rye bread, or as a sandwich filling... particularly good topping a half of English muffin, covered with a little grated cheese and broiled until cheese melts.

Coffee and Brandy Sponge Cake

This is a light dessert cake, very nice to serve with ice cream and coffee when you have friends in for the evening. For those who are weight-conscious this is an ideal dessert because, as a sponge cake, it does not contain butter or shortening.

Yield: About 12 servings
Oven setting: 325 degrees Fahrenheit

- **1/2 cup cold strong coffee**
- **1/4 cup brandy**
- **3 eggs, separated**
- **3/4 cup brown sugar**
- **3/4 cup cake flour**
- **1 tsp baking powder**

Mix the coffee and brandy. Add the egg yolks one at a time and beat after each one is added. Gradually add the sugar while continuing to beat. Continue to beat at medium speed of your electric mixer for an additional 4 minutes after the sugar is added.

In a separate bowl combine the cake flour and baking powder.

In a third bowl beat the egg whites until they are stiff enough to hold a peak when the beater is removed.

Slowly add the flour to the egg mixture while stirring. Gently fold the beaten egg whites into the batter. Be sure to use a U-shaped motion to fold the whites in so that you capture as much air as possible.

Carefully pour into the 9-inch ungreased tube pan and bake at 325 degrees Fahrenheit for about 45 minutes (test the center of the cake with a probe, if it comes out clean the cake is done). Do not under-bake. Invert the cake onto a cooling rack.

If you like, glaze the cake with the Brandy Glaze on the next page, or serve with whipped cream and a dash of nutmeg.

Brandy Glaze

- **2 tbsp butter/margarine**
- **1 cup powdered sugar**
- **2 tbsp brandy**

Melt the butter/margarine and remove from heat. Stir in the brandy and beat in the powdered sugar. The frosting should be on the thin side so that you can pour it rather than spreading it. Pour over the top of the cake and along the edge of the cake top so that it will run down the sides of the cake.

Corn Relish

This is an old-fashioned recipe for corn relish made with fresh corn. It is so good that you'll find a bowl of it disappearing in a single meal. A nice condiment to serve with beef or ham, and also with cold cuts. It makes a pretty addition to a buffet too.

Yield: About 6 pints

    12 ears of corn
    2 stalks of celery
    2 green bell peppers
    2 red bell peppers
    1 large onion
    1 tbsp celery seed
    1 tbsp salt
    1 tbsp turmeric
    1 tbsp mustard seed
    1 tbsp dry mustard
    2 cups water
    2 cups white vinegar
    1 cup sugar

(See "Canning Using a Boiling Water Bath Process" on page 29 for complete information on how to process the Corn Relish for long-term storage.)

In a kettle large enough to hold the corn, bring water to a boil. Remove the husks and silk from the corn and add the corn, all at one time, to the boiling water. Cook for 5 minutes. While the corn cooks prepare a large bowl of ice water. When the corn is cooked, remove the ears from the boiling water and immediately plunge them into the ice water to stop the cooking.

When cool, remove from the water and cut the kernels from the cobs. You should have about 2 quarts of kernels for this recipe.

Chop the celery, green and red peppers, and onion into very small pieces. In a large kettle combine the corn kernels, chopped vegetables, spices, water, vinegar, and sugar. Bring to a boil and then reduce heat and cook, uncovered, for 20 minutes. Stir from time to time. This will make a thinnish sort of liquid with the relish. If you prefer a thickened sauce, simply combine 2 tbsp flour with 1/4 cup water and mix until lump-free then add the flour-water combination to the boiling relish.

Process in a boiling water bath for 15 minutes. (See page 29.)

Cornbread Mix

This is a very handy mix to keep in your refrigerator to use to whip up a pan of fragrant cornbread quickly any time. Although mainly used to make cornbread and cornmeal muffins, you can also be used to make spoon bread and tamale pie.

It is a mix that makes a nice gift too... you might put it in a decorated container and present it with a muffin pan or perhaps one of those lovely cast iron molds that bake in the shape of ears of corn.

Yield: About 10 cups of dry mix

4 cups all-purpose flour
1 tbsp salt
1 cup sugar
4 tbsp baking powder
1 cup shortening
4 cups yellow cornmeal

Combine the flour, salt, sugar, and baking powder in a large bowl. Add the shortening and cut it in with a pastry blender (or use your mixer or food processor for the job). Add the cornmeal last and mix it in well. Store in an airtight container in your refrigerator. It will keep well for about 3-4 months.

To make cornbread or muffins:
Combine 2 1/2 cups of cornbread mix with 1 lightly beaten egg and 1 1/4 cup milk. Mix until just blended (don't over-mix). Pour into greased 8x8-inch pan or muffin pan and bake at 425 degrees Fahrenheit for about 25 minutes (less for muffins).

Cottage Cheese Dumplings (Topfenknodel)

This dish from Austria, which is called Topfenknodel there, goes well with a light lunch and also can be served with fruit for brunch or dessert.

Yield: 2 to 3 servings

1/4 cup butter (use butter not margarine for this)
2 eggs separated
1 1/2 cups dry curd cottage cheese
1/2 tsp salt
1 cup flour (or more depending on size of eggs)
Melted butter

Melt 1/4 cup butter and stir into egg yolks until creamy. Scoop the dry curd cottage cheese into your blender or food processor and make into a puree. Blend into egg yolk mixture with salt. Beat egg whites until they will hold a peak and fold gently into the cheese mixture. Add enough flour to make stiff batter. Bring a deep pan of water to a gentle boil and add 1 tsp salt. Drop dumplings into boiling water and cook until they rise to the surface. Drain and serve with melted butter.

Cranberry Compote

Cranberry Compote is something worth having on hand from Thanksgiving all the way through New Year's Day. It goes wonderfully well with turkey, game, and ham. It does equally well as a sauce for puddings, a filling for tarts, or a topping on ice cream. Truly a versatile recipe.

Yield: about 2 cups

> 1 12-ounce package of fresh or frozen cranberries
> 1 cup orange juice
> 1 cup sugar
> 1 cup peeled and diced cooking apple (such as Granny Smith)
> 1 orange peeled and cut into small pieces

Wash the berries and put them in a medium-sized saucepan. Add the orange juice and sugar. Bring quickly to a boil over high heat and then reduce the heat. Add diced apples and orange pieces. Cook until all of the cranberries have burst and the apples are transparent. Cool. This can also be frozen.

Cream Cheese Pound Cake

This pound cake has a smoother "crumb" than most. It keeps very well in the refrigerator and you can slice it into very thin slices. It is somewhat bland in flavor and takes well to fruit toppings. You can divide the cake into parts, wrap in foil and keep in the freezer until you need a quick dessert some evening.

Yield: 10-inch cake that will serve 8 to 10
Oven setting: 325 degrees Fahrenheit

- 1 cup butter/margarine
- 8 ounces cream cheese
- 3 cups sugar
- 6 eggs
- 3 cups cake flour
- 1 1/2 tsp vanilla extract
- 1/2 tsp almond extract or 1 tsp lemon extract
- Powdered sugar

Preheat oven to 325 degrees Fahrenheit.

Butter a 10 x 4-inch tube pan or a Bundt pan and dust it with flour.

Soften butter/margarine and cream cheese. Cream them together and add sugar one cup at a time and beat until creamy and smooth. Add eggs one at a time and beat well after adding each one. Stir in the flour. Add flavorings.

Pour the batter into the prepared pan and bake for about 1 1/4 hour or until cake tester comes out clean when center of cake is checked.

Cool in pan for 10 minutes then turn upside down on a cake rack and carefully remove from the pan. Sprinkle with powdered sugar while still warm.

Crunchy Coating for Chicken, Fish, or Pork

This is a staple mix that you will always want to have in your cupboard because it is so versatile. It is easy to make up a double or even triple batch at one time and simple store until you use it, which you will do in a surprisingly short time.

Yield: About 2 cups of coating

1 cup corn meal
1/2 cup grated Parmesan cheese
1/4 cup toasted sesame seed
1/2 cup fine cereal flake crumbs
1 tbsp garlic powder
1 tbsp dry parsley flakes
1 tbsp dry savory leaves
1 tbsp crumbled dry sage
1 tsp salt
1/2 tsp pepper

Mix together well and store in jar with tight lid.

For oven-fried chicken:

Yield: Serves 4 (one whole chicken or an assortment of pieces)
Oven setting: 400 degrees Fahrenheit

2 tbsp butter/margarine
2 tbsp oil
1 cup coating mix
2 eggs
1 tbsp water
1/4 cup flour

Heat oven to 400 degrees Fahrenheit. Put butter/margarine and oil in shallow pan (10x15-inch jelly-roll pan is ideal) and place in oven until butter/margarine melts. Meanwhile put coating mix in a shallow bowl. Mix the eggs and water and put in another shallow bowl. Put flour in a third bowl. Rinse chicken pieces and pat dry. Roll each piece in flour, then dip in egg mixture and then coat thoroughly with coating mix. Place each piece on baking pan then turn so that buttered side is up. Arrange pieces so they do not touch. Bake at 400 degrees Fahrenheit for 1 hour (turn pieces after half hour).

For oven-fried fish:

Yield: Serves 4-6 depending on size of fish pieces
Oven setting: 450 degrees Fahrenheit

Use firm white fish and cut into serving size pieces. Proceed as above but bake at 450 degrees Fahrenheit for about 10 minutes or until fish flakes easily.

For oven-fried pork:

Yield: Serves 6
Oven setting: 400 degrees Fahrenheit

Use thin cut pork chops. Proceed as for chicken. Bake at 400 degrees Fahrenheit for about 30 minutes.

Cullen Skink

Dishes with unusual names are always fun to fix for family and guests. This rather wild sounding name belongs to a fairly simple, but very good, fish chowder that is made with smoked fish. It comes from Scotland, home of grand fish dishes as well as dishes with strange names! (Incidentally, "skink" is an old Gaelic word that means "essence", but is commonly used to mean a broth or soup.)

Yield: 8 servings

- **1 pound potatoes**
- **1 large onion**
- **1 pound smoked haddock** (finnan haddie)
- **2 cups milk**
- **1/2 cup butter** (butter is best in this recipe)

Peel the potatoes and dice into 1/2 inch pieces. Chop the onion into small pieces too and add both to 4 quarts of water in a large pan. Bring to a boil and simmer until potatoes are tender (about 10 minutes). While the vegetables are cooking, break the fish up into smallish sized chunks and cut the butter into pieces too. When the vegetables are cooked, add the finnan haddie pieces, the milk, and the butter. Bring the mixture back to a boil then reduce the heat and simmer for 5 minutes. Taste and add salt if you need it. Serve in heated bowl with a dusting of fresh ground pepper and a pat of butter floating on top.

Curry Powder

In India, the birthplace of curry, there is no such thing as a "curry powder". There cooks blend spices that are appropriate for each individual dish they are preparing.

In fact, the word "curry" is not Indian. It has been explained as the British version of the word which means sauce in South Indian Tamil language, and also taken from spicy kari leaf which is a common ingredient.

Nevertheless, here is a recipe for "curry powder", one that will work well in most recipes calling for that ingredient. It is better than most store-bought curry powders and one that you can vary to suit your own taste too.

Yield: About 1/4 cup

   10 whole black peppercorns
   2-inch piece of whole cinnamon stick
   1 tsp whole fenugreek seeds*
   1/2 tsp whole allspice
   10 whole cloves
   1/2 tsp ground turmeric
   1/2 tsp ground cumin
   1/2 tsp ground nutmeg

In your blender grind the whole spices together. Add the powdered spices. Store in an air-tight container in a dry place.

*A good place to find fenugreek seeds is a health food store.

Curry Seasoning Oil

Curry oil is often useful to have on hand. It can be used when sauteing fish or chicken to add flavor. It can be used as part of the oil in an oil-and-vinegar salad dressing. It can be shaken on vegetables instead of using butter or margarine. (It's particularly good on cauliflower and other "strong" flavored vegetables.)

Yield: About 1/4 cup flavored oil

6 tbsp curry powder
1 tsp ground cumin
2 tbsp fresh ginger chopped
1 tsp ground coriander
2 tsp dried mint leaves
1/2 tsp ground cloves
1 tbsp turmeric
1 tbsp fresh ground pepper
1/2 tsp allspice
1 large clove garlic crushed
1/2 cup mild cooking oil (such as sunflower)
1/4 cup sesame oil

Mix dry ingredients together. Add oil to mixture and pour all into a heavy skillet (cast iron is perfect). Over low heat, heat the mixture until it just bubbles, stir constantly but gently for about 3 minutes. Remove from heat and allow to cool to room temperature without further stirring. Strain through a sieve into a jar with a tight cover and store in the refrigerator. Use within about 6 months.

Some other uses for curry oil include using in curry sauces of course, but also use to saute rice for a pilaf; add a tbsp to each pound of lean ground beef for a slightly different flavor when making burger steaks; add to medium thick white sauce to use on vegetables and to thin white sauce when making creamed soups (specially good with cauliflower, carrots, or broccoli).

Dill Dip

This dip is universally popular. The recipe makes a great deal of dip, a full quart, but you will find that there will be none left at the end of the party. It is as good with chilled vegetable pieces as it is with the more traditional chips too. In fact, thinned with a little water to pouring consistency, Dill Dip makes a good salad dressing.

Yield: 4 cups dip

2 cups sour cream
2 cups mayonnaise
3 tbsp grated onion
3-5 tbsp dried dill, to your preference
3 tbsp finely minced fresh parsley
2 tsp seasoning salt (purchased or make your own)
1 tsp worcestershire sauce

Mix all ingredients. (If time allows, make a few hours before dip is to be used to allow flavors to blend.) Serve with thick potato chips or chilled vegetable crudites as "dippers".

Dundee Cake

This is almost a fruitcake, but not quite. It has all the standard ingredients we associate with fruitcakes, but is much lighter. This might be the fruitcake for people who don't like fruitcake. It is a dessert that you can serve all year round and not limit to just the holiday season.

The name, by the way, refers to the city of Dundee in Scotland. In Scotland and England it is often served with afternoon tea.

Yield: 16 servings
Oven setting: 350 degrees Fahrenheit

1 cup butter (use butter for this recipe,
    not margarine)
1 cup sugar
5 eggs
1 1/2 cups cake flour (all-purpose can be used,
    if necessary)
1/2 cup ground almonds
1/2 cup currants
1/2 cup golden raisins
1/2 cup diced mixed candied fruit
2 tbsp grated orange zest
1 tsp baking soda
1 tsp milk
1/3 cup whole almonds, blanched

Prepare an 8-inch spring-form pan by buttering well and then dusting with flour.

If you have an electric mixer, it is useful in preparing the batter. Mix the butter and sugar together until they are creamy, smooth, and light. Add the eggs one at a time and beat well after adding each one. With the beater at low speed, add the flour and mix well.

In a separate bowl, combine the ground almonds, currants, raisins, diced fruit, and orange peel. By hand, mix these ingredients into the batter. Mix the baking powder with the milk and add to the batter. Pour the assembled batter into the spring form pan and arrange the whole blanched almonds on the top of the cake.

Bake for about 1 1/2 hours or until a cake tester comes out clean when inserted in the center of the cake (cake will also pull away from the pan slightly when done). Remove from the spring-form pan and cool on a rack. It is best if you allow this cake to rest until completely cooled before cutting into slices to serve.

Dutch Babies

The origin of the name for this dish is an intriguing mystery. Basically Dutch Babies are a variation of a baked pancake, and they have been a Northwest favorite for generations. Dutch Babies were a specialty at a restaurant in Seattle called Manca's which, alas, is no longer on the scene but remembered with nostalgia by old-timers in the area.

This makes a nice dessert after a simple supper but you should plan to serve it right from the oven because it doesn't hold well.

Yield: 4-6 servings depending on the size of appetites
Oven setting: 400 degrees Fahrenheit

3 eggs
1/2 cup flour
1/2 cup milk
1/2 tsp salt
2 tbsp melted butter (for best flavor use butter not margarine)
Butter
Lemon wedges
Powdered sugar

Beat the eggs until they are light and fluffy. Add the flour to the eggs about 2 tablespoons at a time (so you add it in 4 parts). Beat after each addition so that the batter is smooth. Add the milk the same way, in 4 parts beating after each addition. Add the melted butter and salt and beat again.

Put a generous coating of butter on each of two 9-inch pie pans. Pour half of the batter into each buttered pie pan and bake at 400 degrees for 10 minutes. Reduce oven heat to 350 and bake for 5 minutes more. Remove from oven and sprinkle with powdered sugar. Cut into serving size pieces and serve immediately with additional butter and lemon wedges. You can also offer some fresh fruit such as strawberries or cooked apple slices to go with the Dutch Babies.

Egg Roll Wrappers

This sort of very unleavened dough is found in many cultures from the fila of the Middle East to this Oriental version. Although egg roll wrappers are more easily available now in most locations than they once were, you may be someplace where they are not easily accessible. You may also simply prefer to make them yourself. For whatever reason, here is the recipe.

Yield: 48 wrappers

4 cups sifted all purpose flour
2 tsp salt
2 eggs
1 cup ice water
Cornstarch

Sift flour and salt into large bowl. Make a well in the center and add eggs and water. Using a fork, stir the dough until it just holds together and leaves the sides of the bowl. Turn out onto a floured surface and knead until smooth and elastic (about 5 minutes or, if you prefer, use the dough hook on your mixer or food processor. Cover the dough and allow to rest for at least 30 minutes.

Divide the dough into four parts. Dust your pastry board lightly with cornstarch and roll each piece of dough out to an 11x14-inch rectangle. Cut the 14-inch length into four parts and the 11-inch length into three parts (you will have 12 3 1/2-inch squares of dough. Stack on a plate (the cornstarch will prevent sticking). Repeat with the remaining three parts of dough.

If you are not going to use right away, wrap securely and freeze.

Eggnog Pie

Here is a dessert that is not too heavy to be served after a holiday dinner, but also is able to stand on its own for a coffee-and-dessert get-together. This is a desert that benefits greatly from using freshly grated nutmeg, always better than pre-ground but in Eggnog Pie it is almost a necessity.

Yield: 8 servings
Oven setting: 400 degrees Fahrenheit

For the shell:

1 cup all-purpose flour
1 tbsp sugar
1/4 tsp salt
1/3 cup vegetable shortening
iced water

For the filling:

1 envelope of unflavored gelatin
2 cups milk
1 tbsp cornstarch
1/4 tsp salt
6 tbsp sugar
2 eggs, separated
2-4 tbsp brandy or rum to your taste
(In this recipe the liquor is added after the filling is cooked so the alcohol is not evaporated. If you prefer not to have alcohol in the dish, you can substitute brandy or rum flavoring extracts.)
Freshly grated nutmeg if possible, otherwise ground nutmeg

Prepare the pie shell:

Combine the flour, sugar and salt in a small bowl and then cut in the shortening using a pastry blender. When the mixture resembles coarse cornmeal, add about 1/4 cup of ice water and using your hands, but working the dough as little as possible (you want it to stay as cold as possible), mix in the water. Add more water if needed to produce a dough that will hold together in a ball.

Roll out to about 1/4 inch and then fold the circle of dough into quarters and place in a 9-inch pie pan. Turn the edges under and, using your thumb and forefinger, press a fluted design into the edge. Using a fork, prick the pastry all over the bottom of the shell and also around the sides. Bake at

400 degrees for about 15 minutes or until golden brown. Remove from oven and cool to room temperature.

Make the filling:

Sprinkle the gelatin over 1/2 cup of the milk, stir it in gently and allow it to soften. In the top portion of a double boiler combine the cornstarch, salt and 3 tbsp of the sugar and add the rest of the milk and the egg yolks which have been slightly beaten. Stirring constantly, cook over simmering water until the mixture thickens. Remove from heat, cover and allow to rest for 10 minutes.

Stir the gelatin mixture into the thickened milk mixture. Return to the heat and cook for 5 minutes while you stir constantly. Remove from the heat. Cover and place in the refrigerator to cool until chilled.

Beat the egg whites until frothy and add the rest of the sugar as you beat until they become quite firm. Add the brandy or rum (or extracts) to the chilled thickened milk mixture. Fold in the beaten egg whites. Pour into the cooled pie shell and sprinkle nutmeg on the top. Chill at least 1 hour before serving.

Italian Eggplant Casserole

Eggplant is a rather undervalued vegetable. Pretty to look at, but not much prized for flavor. What it needs is some help... and this casserole gives it plenty of that. Try it out without revealing what the main ingredient is and see how many people can recognize the eggplant...

Yield: Serves 6
Oven setting: 350 degrees Fahrenheit

- 1/2 cup olive oil
- 1/2 cup finely chopped onion
- 2 cloves of garlic, finely minced
- 2 8-ounce cans of tomato sauce
- 1 tsp dried basil
- 1/2 tsp dried oregano
- 1 tsp sugar
- 1/2 tsp ground pepper
- 1 large eggplant (1 to 1 1/2 pounds)
- 1 egg
- 1/4 cup milk
- 1 cup dried bread crumbs
- 8 ounces mozzarella cheese
- 8 ounces ricotta cheese
- 1/2 cup Parmesan cheese, freshly grated if possible

In a large skillet, heat 1/4 cup of the olive oil and saute the onions and garlic until tender. In a sauce pan combine the cooked onions and garlic with the tomato sauce, basil, sugar and pepper. Bring to a boil then reduce heat and simmer for 20 minutes.

While the sauce is cooking, pare the eggplant and slice it lengthwise into thin slices (about 1/4 inch thick). In a shallow bowl, beat the egg with the milk. Put the bread crumbs in a second shallow bowl. Dip each piece of eggplant into the egg-milk mixture and then coat with the crumbs. Place the coated pieces on a rack.

Add the remaining 1/4 cup of olive oil to the skillet used to saute the onions and garlic. Heat the oil and saute the eggplant pieces until they are golden brown.

Put about 1/3 of the sauce into a 8x8-inch baking pan.

Shred the mozzarella cheese and mix it with the ricotta. Put a generous teaspoonful of the cheese mixture in the middle of each eggplant slice and roll up. Place with seam side down in the tomato sauce in the pan. Cover with the tomato sauce and sprinkle the top with grated Parmesan.

Bake at 350 degrees for 30 minutes.

Chinese Five-Spice Powder

Although Oriental condiments and spices are far easier to find now that several years ago, sometimes five-spice is not easy to locate. It is quite simple to make, probably less expensive to make than buy too. You will find Chinese recipes frequently call for it, but don't limit its use to Oriental dishes... you'll find it called for in a chicken breast recipe on page 44.

Yield: About 1/3 cup

    2 tbsp whole black peppercorns
    45 whole cloves
    10-12 inches of whole cinnamon stick
    2 tbsp fennel seed
    12 whole star anise

Simply put all of the whole spices in your blender and grind together. Store in an air-tight container in a dry place.

Flavoring Extracts

It is not a bit difficult to make your own natural flavoring extracts. The result is a more delicate flavor than store-bought, at a much lower cost. It also means that you can have a never-ending supply on hand.

Vanilla Extract:

Vanilla Bean
Vodka

It is best to use a brown-glass bottle to prepare vanilla extract. You can purchase one from your pharmacy if you don't have one on hand that you can recycle. Cut the vanilla bean into several long pieces that will fit into the bottle. Fill the bottle with vodka. Allow it to steep for 4 weeks, shaking from time to time. After you have used about a quarter of the bottle, add enough additional vodka to fill the bottle again.

Lemon/Orange/Lime Extract:

Lemons (oranges or limes)
Vodka

Use well-colored fruit and remove strips of the zest. (The outer colored portion of the peel... do not include any of the white pithy part.) You will probably be happier using a wider mouthed bottle to make citrus extracts. Put the zest in the bottle (until it is about one-third filled with zest) then fill the bottle with vodka. Allow it to steep for 2 weeks, shaking form time to time. This extract can not be replenished in the way you can vanilla extract so after 2 weeks, pour the extract through a fine sieve into a brown-glass bottle and discard the zests.

Frozen Fruit Salad

Food fads come and go as you have no doubt noticed. There was a time when molded salads were very popular, and frozen fruit salads were one of the most popular of all. They are good enough to deserve a second look... if nothing more than to remind ourselves of the "comfort foods" of the past.

Yield: 8 servings

2 eggs
1 8-ounce can of crushed pineapple
1 8-ounce can of apricot halves
1/3 cup sugar
3 tbsp lemon juice
1/8 tsp salt
2 cup whipping cream
1 cup sliced fresh strawberries (in the winter you can use
    canned cherries)
1 cup shredded cheddar cheese
1/2 cup chopped walnuts
Lettuce leaves

Oil a 6-cup ring mold or 6 individual molds.

Beat eggs until frothy. In a saucepan combine undrained crushed pineapple with 2 tbsp liquid from canned apricot halves, beaten eggs, sugar, lemon juice and salt. Over moderate heat, cook the mixture, stirring constantly, until it thickens (it should not boil). Remove from the heat and allow to cool, stirring from time to time. Drain apricot halves and cut each half into two parts.

When the pineapple mixture has cooled, beat the cream until it will hold a soft peak when the beaters are removed and then fold the beaten cream into the pineapple mixture. Fold in the apricots, sliced strawberries (or cherries), shredded cheese and chopped nuts. Pour the mixture into the mold (or molds) and freeze until firm. To serve, unmold onto a serving plate and place in the refrigerator until ready to serve. (It will hold for about 3 hours in the refrigerator.)

Baked Fruit Squares

This is a great dessert to take with you on picnics or when you volunteer to bring dessert for a party. It makes quite a large cake. You can vary the fruit filling that is used although the cherry filling is colorful as well as flavorful. Best of all, this is a dessert that is quick and easy to make.

Yield: 10x15-inch pan... about 15 servings
Oven setting: 350 degrees Fahrenheit

1 1/2 cup sugar
1 cup butter (use butter, not margarine for this recipe)
4 eggs
2 cups cake flour (use all-purpose flour only if you have to)
1/2 tsp salt
1 tbsp lemon juice
1 tbsp grated lemon zest
1 cup prepared cherry pie filling (or other flavor if you prefer)
Powdered sugar

Grease and dust with flour a 10x15-inch (jelly roll) baking pan.

Mix the sugar and butter together until they are creamy, smooth and light. (An electric mixer works very well for this.) Add eggs one at a time and beat the mixture well after adding each egg. Add the flour, salt, lemon juice, and grated lemon zest while beating at low speed. Pour the batter into the prepared pan.

With the back of a table knife, mark the surface into 15 squares (3 marks lengthwise and 5 across). Place a heaping tablespoon of pie filling in the center of each square. Bake at 350 degrees Fahrenheit for 45-50 minutes. While the cake is still warm, sift some powdered sugar over the top.

Cool and cut into squares to serve.

Garam Masala

If you ever become interested in the intriguing food of India, you are sure to run across recipes calling for Garam Masala.

"Masala" is a word used in India to indicate a mixture of spices. The mixture may be either a paste or a dry mix. Garam Masala is probably the most widely used spice blend. It is a spicy mixture used in many Indian dishes, probably the one westerners are most familiar with is Tandoori Chicken, that great barbecued chicken dish from India.

In some locations, it is not always easy to find Garam Masala and this recipe will allow you to make your own... with the added advantage that it will be fresh.

Yield: About 2 tbsp
Oven setting: 450 degrees Fahrenheit

2 tsp ground cardamom
1 tsp ground cumin
1/2 tsp ground cinnamon
1/4 tsp ground cloves
1/4 tsp ground nutmeg
1/4 tsp ground pepper
1/4 tsp ground coriander
(The amounts can be increased, just keep the proportions the same.)

Combine the spices and place on a cookie sheet or other flat pan in the oven for no more than 3 minutes. Remove, cool and stir. Store in an air-tight container. This will keep for several months.

In addition to classic Indian dishes, Garam Masala can also be used to perk up soups (particularly creamed soups), stews, and in vegetable casseroles.

Roasted Garlic

Does the thought of eating roasted whole cloves of garlic seem strange? That's not surprising, but once you try them, you will be surprised at how mild the garlic taste can become.

These baked garlic heads are surprisingly versatile too... you can use them as a condiment when serving steaks or roast beef, they are also interesting to use mashed as an appetizer spread, and try them mixed with butter/margarine and serve with steamed new potatoes (or other vegetables)

Yield: Depends on size of garlic heads
Oven setting: 325 degrees Fahrenheit

Whole heads of garlic

Take the outer coverings away from each head of garlic, but leave the head intact. Place it (or them) on a shallow pan that has been lightly oiled. Bake at 325 degrees Fahrenheit for 1 hour, the cloves will yield to pressure when they are done. Allow to cool and then remove the individual cloves and squeeze them to slip them out of their coverings.

Graham Crackers

Memories of childhood almost always carry nostalgia about that quintessential childhood-treat combination: milk-and-graham crackers.

The graham cracker was developed, perhaps you might even say "invented", by Dr. Sylvester Graham who lived in the early 1800's. Dr. Graham called them "Health Crackers" because their ingredients were all simple and wholesome.

This version is a little more elaborate that the original wheat flour, bran, and molasses wafer, but will taste more like what we think of as Dr. Graham's Crackers.

Yield: varies depending on size of the cut crackers
Oven setting: 375 degrees Fahrenheit

1/4 cup powdered milk
1/2 cup water
2 tbsp lemon juice
2 eggs
1 cup brown sugar
1/2 cup honey
1 cup mild vegetable oil
2 tsp vanilla extract
1 tsp salt
1 tsp baking soda
6 cups whole wheat flour

Mix the powdered milk and water together and then add the lemon juice and mix. In a separate bowl, beat the eggs until light and then add the brown sugar, honey, oil, and vanilla extract. Stir the salt and baking soda into 3 cups of the flour and combine with egg mixture. Continue to add flour until the dough is very stiff.

Divide the dough into 4 parts. Lightly grease a cookie sheet with shortening and dust it with flour. Roll one part of the dough out on the cookie sheet until it is about 1/8 inch thick. Lightly mark out squares with a blunt knife and use a fork to prick the squares every inch or so. Bake about 15 minutes until lightly browned.

Cut into squares immediately and move to a cooling rack.

Repeat with the other 3 parts of the dough.

Spiced Grape Butter

There is something about the redolence of the rich aroma of ripe grapes that can make your mouth water just to think about it. When you combine that fruit-sweet taste with some spices the combination is superb. Spiced Grape Butter is good as an accompaniment to turkey, pork and ham as well as being a delicious jam anytime. It is another of those special preserves that makes a lovely gift.

Yield: about 4 half-pints

  8 generous cups of stemmed purple Concord grapes
    (about 4 pounds)
  1/2 cup white vinegar (white wine vinegar is best)
  4 1/2 cups sugar
  1/2 tsp ground allspice
  1/2 tsp ground cinnamon
  1/2 tsp ground cloves

(See "Canning Using a Boiling Water Bath Process" on page 29 for complete information on how to process Spiced Grape Butter for long-term storage.)

Remove skins from grapes by pinching the grape and forcing the pulp out. Put the skins in a pan with enough water to just barely cover and cook for 30 minutes stirring from time to time to keep fruit from sticking to bottom of the pan). Force the pulp of the grapes through a sieve to remove seeds (or use a food mill if you have one).

Add pureed pulp to skins with sugar, vinegar, allspice, cinnamon, and cloves and stir until sugar is well distributed and partly dissolved.

Bring to a gentle boil and cook until mixture has thickened to your taste. (This should take 30 to 45 minutes.)

Pour into sterilized jars. Process in a boiling water bath for 5 minutes. (See page 29.)

Stuffed Grape Leaves

This appetizer is popular in Greece, Turkey, and other parts of the Middle East. Allow yourself ample preparation time because they do take a bit of time to make. Stuffed grape leaves can be used as finger-food for a cocktail party, or 3 or 4 can be arranged on a plate as an appetizer course.

Yield: About 50 small grape leaf rolls

1 cup olive oil
2 cups finely chopped onion
1 1/2 tsp salt
1/2 tsp pepper
2 cups raw long grained rice
2 tbsp dried dill
1 cup chopped parsley
12 green onions including tops
1/2 cup lemon juice
One lemon cut in slices
1-2 bottles prepared grape leaves

Heat oil and saute onions until limp and golden. Add salt, pepper, and rice. Lightly saute rice so that it is well coated with oil. Add 1/2 cup water, cover and cook for 10 minutes. Add dill, chopped parsley, chopped green onions, lemon juice and 1 cup water. Cook 10 minutes more.

While filling is cooking, remove grape leaves from jars and unroll them carefully. Put the dull, veined side of the leaves up and when the filling is ready, place a spoonful on each leaf. To roll, fold the sides of the leaves over and then roll up starting at the stem. Place the rolls, seam side down, in a large pan that has a tight cover. On top of each layer of grape leaf rolls scatter some of the lemon slices.

When all the rolls have been arranged in the pan, place a plate on top of the rolls to weight them down. Pour about 4 cups of water over the rolls, cover tightly and bring to a gentle boil. Simmer for 25 minutes.

Cool in the pan and then very carefully remove to a serving plate or tray and store in the refrigerator until served.

These can be made a day ahead and keep nicely.

Green Pepper Jelly

This can be used in a variety of ways... as an accessory to meat it is particularly good with pork and lamb. It also tastes delicious with cream cheese and crackers as a snack.

Yield: About 4 half-pint jars

6 large green peppers
1 1/2 cups cider vinegar
6 cups sugar
1/2 tsp cayenne pepper
1/2 tsp salt
6 ounces liquid pectin
Green food coloring
Paraffin

Remove stems, seeds and white portions of peppers and cut into pieces about an inch square. Put half of the peppers and half the vinegar in a blender or food processor and puree. Repeat with remaining peppers and vinegar. Put the puree into a large pan and add sugar, cayenne, and salt.

Stir constantly while you bring mixture to a full rolling boil and add liquid pectin. Continue to boil for 1 minute, stirring constantly.

Remove from heat and stir in enough green food coloring to achieve a green that you find satisfactory.

Pour immediately into sterilized jelly jars and seal with a thin layer of melted paraffin. Store in a cool dry place.

Whole Wheat Hamburger Buns

Let's face it, we all love hamburgers. By making these whole wheat buns to go with the burgers, you will be giving a little extra nutrition in a very unobtrusive way. These buns also hold together better than the somewhat flimsy buns you can buy. The rolls do not take long to make especially if you have an electric mixer with a dough hook or a food processor to help with the kneading.

Yield: 10 buns
Oven setting: 425 degrees Fahrenheit

1 1/4 cups warm water (about 100 degrees Fahrenheit)
1/3 cup mild oil
1/4 cup sugar (or honey)
2 pkgs of yeast (2 scant tbsp)
4 tsp salt
1 egg yolk
2 1/2 cups whole wheat flour
1 cup bread flour (or all-purpose flour)
Melted butter/margarine

Combine water, oil, sugar and yeast. Mix thoroughly and then allow to rest for 15 minutes. Mix in the salt, egg yolk, whole wheat flour, and white flour and combine until thoroughly mixed (at least 10 minutes). On a floured board, roll the dough out to until it is about 3/4-inch thick. Cut circles of dough about 4-inches in diameter with a cutter (or use an large empty can that you have washed out).

Place the buns on a cookie sheet, brush the tops with melted butter/margarine, and allow to raise for 30 minutes.

Bake at 425 degrees Fahrenheit for 10 minutes or until golden brown.

Herring in Sour Cream

Herring in sour cream sauce can be purchased in the cooler case of most supermarkets but somehow those little bottles are just too small for people who really like this Scandinavian delicacy. With this recipe you can inexpensively make as much as you need for a special first course appetizer.

Yield: 6 to 8 servings

1 pound pickled herring pieces
1 cup sour cream
3 tbsp lemon juice
1 large mild onion sliced paper thin
1 tsp very coarsely ground black pepper
1 tsp salt

Drain liquid from herring pieces. Mix remaining ingredients together and gently stir in the herring and turn to coat all pieces with the sour cream sauce. Cover and store in refrigerator for at least 2 hrs. before serving. These should be used within 4 days.

Garnish with thin lemon slices and/or paprika and serve with thin slices of pumpernickel bread or rye crackers.

Hominy Casserole

Hominy is not the most popular of vegetables but it has a distinctive flavor that stands up to meats well. This particular casserole is good to serve with barbecued meats. It also travels for picnics and can be a nice addition to a buffet table.

Yield: 8 servings
Oven setting: 400 degrees Fahrenheit

3 cups canned hominy (2 cans of about 1 1/2 cups each)
1 tbsp mild cooking oil (such as corn or sunflower)
1/2 cup finely chopped onion
1/2 cup finely chopped green pepper
1 fresh tomato, chopped (about 1/2 cup)
1/2 pound cheddar or jack cheese, shredded (about 2 cups)
1/2 chili powder
1/4 tsp ground cumin
1 fresh tomato to slice for garnish
1/4 cup chopped parsley

Saute the chopped onion and chopped green pepper in oil until tender. Rinse the canned hominy and put into a large bowl. Add the sauteed onions and green pepper.

Peel the tomato, squeeze out the seeds and chop. Add chopped tomato, grated cheese, chili powder, and cumin and mix well.

Pour into an oiled baking dish that has a cover. Cover and bake at 400 degrees for about 30 minutes until thoroughly heated.

Peel the second tomato and cut into thin slices. Arrange the slices on top of the casserole and scatter chopped parsley over all.

Honey Jelly

This is a lovely, mellow flavored jelly. If you use a heavier flavored honey, the honey flavor will predominate. If you use a simple honey (supermarkets usually carry clover honey), the apple flavor will be a little more noticeable. In either case, you'll like it.

Yield: About 3 half pints

1 3/4 cups honey
1 cup clear apple juice
1 tbsp lemon juice
3 ounces of liquid pectin
Paraffin

Combine the honey, apple juice and lemon juice in a large pan. Bring the mixture quickly to a boil over high heat and stir in the liquid pectin. Bring to a full boil (one that cannot be stirred down) and boil for exactly 1 minute. Remove from heat and stir. Skim off any foam that appears on the top.

Pour into sterilized jars and seal with a thin layer of paraffin. Store in a cool dry place.

Horseradish-Mayonnaise Spread/Sauce

Once you make this up and try it, you'll never be without it. Use it for sandwiches, on meats, with cheeses, on crackers, as a dip for vegetables, and a variety of other things. The amounts of the ingredients can be varied to suit your taste. Best of all, it is very inexpensive to make, calls for no exotic ingredients, and keeps well in your refrigerator.

Yield: Slightly more than a cup of spread

1 cup mayonnaise
3-4 tsp prepared horseradish
2 tsp Dijon-style mustard
1 tsp garlic powder
1 tsp onion powder

Mix all ingredients together and store in a covered container in your refrigerator. Use as a sauce with roast beef or cold cuts. Also as a spread on the bread used to make meat or cheese sandwiches in place of butter or plain mayonnaise.

Hot Buttered Rum Mix

Here's a drink that means winter has arrived. Make this mix up in advance (you can double to make more), and you are all ready for drop in guests who need a warming-up.

Yield: About 3 cups (12 servings)

3 cups brown sugar (1 1/2 pounds)
1/2 cup butter (1/4 pound)
2 tbsp honey
1 tbsp vanilla
1 tbsp rum flavoring
1 tsp ground cinnamon
1/2 tsp ground allspice
1/2 tsp ground nutmeg

Combine brown sugar, butter, honey, flavorings and spices. Beat with an electric mixer at medium speed until smooth. Put in jar with a tight lid. Store in refrigerator and use within 3 months. To make larger amounts just multiply ingredient amounts.

To prepare each serving:

1 cup hot water
1 jigger of rum
1 tsp Hot Buttered Rum Mix

Combine the hot water and rum and stir in about a tsp of the mix.

To make non-alcoholic drink, stir a tsp of mix into other hot beverages: apple juice, hot milk, hot milk mixed with coffee, or plain coffee or tea.

Simple Ice Cream

This is a simple, basic recipe that you make "uncommon" by adding your own personal variations. In a comparison of flavors, fresh home-made ice cream is so much better than anything you can buy that there is hardly any contest at all. Variations in flavor are limited only by your imagination, so let yourself go. The amounts in this recipe is that it make about a quart, just enough for a small group to enjoy... and just the thing for a warm summer evening.

Yield: about 1 quart

2 eggs
2/3 cup sugar
2 cups whipping cream (or half-and-half light cream if you prefer to reduce the calories and saturated fat)
2 cups fruit either pureed, chopped, or mashed (bananas, peaches, any kind of berry, cherries, to make a few possibilities)
1 tsp vanilla extract (or try some almond extract if you are using cherries or peaches)

With an electric mixer, beat the egg and the sugar until they form a thick, light-yellow mixture. Add the pureed fruit, cream and flavorings to the egg mixture and stir until well blended. Process in either a conventional ice cream freezer or in one of the non-electric ice cream makers (such as a *Donvier*) that you chill in your freezer before using. It is possible to make a frozen dessert from this mixture by freezing it in your freezer, but the texture will not be as pleasing. If you do make it without an ice cream maker, stir it from time to time as it freezes.

Ice Ring Frozen with Flowers

A simple-to-make but very decorative frozen flower ring can make a pretty addition to a punch bowl.

Pour a half-inch of water into a ring mold. If you use boiled or distilled water, the ice will be clear when frozen. Freeze for about 3 hours.

Now arrange fresh (or plastic) leaves and flowers with the "good side" down facing the bottom of the mold. Next, very carefully fill the mold with more chilled pre-boiled or distilled water so that the arrangement is not disturbed.

Freeze for 24 hours. This mold can be refrozen and used more than once. Fresh flowers will stay fresh looking as long as they are not exposed to air.

Italian-seasoned Bread Crumbs

Purchased at your store, Italian-seasoned bread crumbs seem a bit expensive considering what they are. You can make your own very easily and very inexpensively. Use them in a variety of ways from breading chicken to topping casseroles.

Yield: About 2 cups of seasoned bread crumbs
Oven setting (if you need to dry bread): 250 degrees Fahrenheit

Leftover bread slices
1/4 cup prepared Parmesan cheese
2 tbsp dried parsley
1 tsp dried oregano
1 tsp dried basil
1 tsp garlic powder
1 tsp onion powder

Save leftover bread and dry it (either out on your counter or in the oven at 250 degrees Fahrenheit for about 15 minutes) until completely dry and crisp.

Using your food processor, blender, or by rolling with a rolling pin between sheets of waxed paper, make fine bread crumbs. Save these crumbs. They are useful in a wide variety of ways.

When you have an ample supply, take out 2 cups and mix with the remaining ingredients noted above.

Store in an air-tight container in your refrigerator and use within 2 months.

Italian "Chili"

Not really Italian, and not really chili, this is, nevertheless, a good dish for those days you would like to have a non-meat main dish. It's filling and flavorful and one that quickly becomes a favorite. So many vegetarian main dishes seem to be a little bland that this spicy mixture is very welcome, and a perfectly acceptable substitute for a meat-oriented meal.

Yield: 8 generous servings

2/3 cup dried black beans
1 medium eggplant
1 tbsp salt
1/2 cup olive oil
1 cup chopped onions
1/2 cup chopped celery
1 cup chopped zucchini
1 large red bell pepper, chopped
1 large yellow bell pepper, chopped
4 cloves of garlic, chopped
4 medium fresh tomatoes (canned may be substituted)
1 cup mixed vegetable juice, tomato juice or water
1 cup chopped parsley
1 tbsp dried basil (1/4 cup chopped fresh)
3 tbsp chili powder
1 tbsp ground cumin
1 tbsp dried oregano
1/2 tsp pepper
1/4-1/2 tsp hot pepper sauce (to taste)
1 pkg frozen corn kernels (1 1/2 cups fresh)
1/2 cup lemon juice

Early in the day or the night before, put the black beans in a large bowl and fill the bowl with water. Soak the beans for several hours and then drain. Put the soaked beans in a large kettle with plenty of water (2 or 3 quarts should do) and bring to a boil. (Do not add salt as that will prevent the beans from softening.) Cook beans until done (about 30 minutes). Check by tasting one to make sure they are tender.

While the beans are cooking, remove the stem and leaves from the eggplant and cut it into small cubes (about 1/2 cubes). Place the cubes in a sieve or colander and sprinkle with the tablespoon of salt. Let it rest for an hour to remove excess moisture from the eggplant and then rinse and pat dry with paper towels.

Heat half of the olive oil in a large heavy skillet and saute the chopped onions, celery, zucchini, peppers and garlic until the onion is golden and translucent (about 10 minutes). Remove from the skillet with a slotted spoon and put into a stove-top safe casserole or Dutch oven.

If needed, add some or all of the rest of the olive oil to the skillet and saute the eggplant cubes until tender (about 5 minutes). Scoop into casserole with other vegetables.

Scald the tomatoes in simmering water for 2 or 3 minutes and quickly in a bowl of cool water to make peeling easier. Cut the peeled tomatoes in half and squeeze them gently to remove the seeds and then chop into 1-inch cubes and add to the casserole.

Add the cup of liquid (vegetable juice or tomato juice is best, water is acceptable if you have neither of the others on hand). Also add half of the parsley, basil, chili powder, cumin, oregano, pepper, and hot pepper sauce. (Taste at this point and add more pepper sauce if you like and also salt if it seems to need it.) Mix well, cover and simmer for 30 minutes, stirring from time to time.

After 30 minutes add the cooked black beans, corn, and lemon juice and cook for 15 minutes more. Taste one more time, you may need to add a little more salt because the beans were not salted, but don't let the salt get out of hand and cover up the vegetable flavors.

Toss the remaining 1/2 cup of chopped parsley on top just before serving. You can also add chopped green onions, grated cheese, and/or sliced black olives to the topping.

Italian Salad Dressing Mix

This mix works equally well with an oil-and-vinegar type dressing or with mayonnaise or yogurt. By using various herb flavored vinegars, you can vary the flavor even more. If you are on a controlled-fat diet, try the mix with just vinegar and no oil.

It is less expensive to make your own mix than it is to buy the small packets of salad dressing mix at the supermarket. Another consideration in making your own is that you can control the amount of salt used. This mix, for instance, does not call for any.

Yield: About 2/3 cup mix

> **1/3 cup dry grated Parmesan** (or Romano) **cheese**
> **1 tbsp garlic powder**
> **1 tbsp onion powder**
> **1 tbsp paprika**
> **1 tbsp celery seeds** (less if you prefer)
> **1 tbsp sesame seeds**

Mix ingredients and store in an air-tight container. Will keep for several months.

To use in an oil-and-vinegar dressing:
Mix 1 tbsp mix with 1/4 cup vinegar, 2 tbsp water, and 2/3 cup oil (or a combination of oils to equal this amount) in a covered container. Shake vigorously.

To use with mayonnaise or yogurt as a salad dressing:
Mix 1 tbsp mix with 1/4 cup mayonnaise and 1 tbsp water in a covered container. Shake vigorously.

To use with mayonnaise, yogurt or sour cream as a dip:
Mix 1 tbsp mix with 1/4 cup of spread. (You can also add some dijon-style mustard and other herbs to your preference.) Serve with raw vegetables.

Joe's Special

Basically, Joe's Special is a variation on a frittata, an egg and vegetable saute of Italian origin. Tradition has it that this great tasting variation of the Italian dish originated in a restaurant in San Francisco but where ever it was created, it certainly is a nice way to eat your spinach.

Yield: 4 generous servings, 6 as a first course

2 tbsp olive oil
2 pounds lean ground beef
1 cup finely chopped onions
3 cloves garlic chopped or mashed
1 cup sliced fresh mushrooms
1 tsp salt
1/2 tsp ground nutmeg
1/2 tsp dried oregano
1/4 tsp coarsely ground pepper
4 cups fresh spinach, washed, blotted and chopped
6 eggs
Parmesan cheese if you like

Heat the olive oil in a skill and cook the ground beef until well browned. Add onions, garlic and mushrooms. Reduce heat and continue to cook while stirring until onions are transparent. Add the salt and other seasonings and the spinach and cook for about 5 minutes (until spinach is limp).

Beat eggs until well mixed but not too frothy and pour over the meat/spinach combination. Cook as you would an omelette by lifting and letting the liquid egg run underneath until eggs are set. An alternative way to finish the dish is to cook the eggs until they are only partially set and then top the mixture with freshly grated parmesan cheese and slip it under your broiler until the cheese melts.

Lemon Buttermilk Pound Cake

This cake is not as smooth as the Cream Cheese Pound Cake, but is more flavorful. It stands on its own because of its lemon flavor. It also is very good toasted.

Yield: 10 to 12 servings
Oven setting: 325 degrees Fahrenheit

3/4 cup water
3/4 cup sugar
3 tbsp lemon juice
3 cups cake flour
1/2 tsp baking soda
1/2 tsp salt
1 cup sweet (unsalted) **butter**
2 cups sugar
5 eggs
1 tsp vanilla extract
1 tbsp lemon juice
1 tbsp grated lemon rind
1 cup buttermilk

Combine water, sugar and lemon juice in a small pan and bring to a boil. Stir until sugar is dissolved and then lower heat and simmer until volume is reduced to half (3/4 to 1 cup remaining). Cool.

Preheat oven to 325 degrees Fahrenheit.

Combine flour, baking soda, and salt. Cream butter and sugar together until light colored. Add eggs one at a time and beat well after adding each one. Add the vanilla extract, lemon juice and grated lemon rind and mix well. Alternately add dry ingredients and then buttermilk until all are combined. Mix well. Butter and thoroughly flour a 10x4-inch tube pan and pour the batter in. Smooth the surface of the batter.

Check with a cake tester after about 1 hour, but cake will probably take 70-80 minutes to completely bake. When tester comes out clean, remove cake from oven and cool, in the pan, on a cake rack for 15 minutes. Turn over and gently remove from pan.

While cake is still warm, brush with the lemon syrup on all sides until syrup has been used up and absorbed by the cake. This is a bit messy so you may want to put a layer of waxed paper down on your counter under the cake rack before you start. Cool cake completely and place on a serving platter.

Lemon Curd

Lemon Curd is a thick, tart-sweet condiment that is very popular in the British Isles. It is a useful recipe to have because it can be used not only for filling small tart shells to make a very pretty dessert, but can also be used anyplace that you would use a fruit butter or thick jam. It is available in gourmet shops and the special import section of many supermarkets, but it is quite expensive to buy and very easy to make.

Yield: About 1 cup

> **1 cup sugar**
> **6 tbsp sweet** (unsalted) **butter**
> **1/3 cup lemon juice**
> **1 tbsp finely grated lemon rind**
> **3 whole eggs plus 1 egg yolk**

In the top of a double boiler, combine the sugar, butter, lemon juice and lemon rind and mix well. Place the pan directly over the heat and, stirring constantly, cook until the sugar is completely dissolved. Remove from heat and cool slightly.

Beat the eggs and the extra egg yolk until light and frothy. Very slowly pour the beaten eggs into the sugar-lemon mixture while you stir constantly.

Bring water to a simmer in the bottom portion of the double boiler and put the upper part of the double boiler in place. Cook over the simmering water, stirring often, until the mixture has thickened (about 20 minutes). The mixture will thicken some more as it cools.

Pour the curd into a covered bowl, or wide-mouthed jar with a lid, and put a layer of plastic wrap on the surface. Cover the container with its lid and chill immediately. When thoroughly chilled, remove the plastic wrap and stir the curd.

It will keep in the refrigerator but should be used within a month so you may wish to put a "use-by" date on the lid.

Lemonade Syrup

In a time when artificial flavors are taken as the norm, you may prefer to make your own "honest" lemonade. This syrup stores well in the refrigerator and allows you to have it on hand all the time during the warm summer months.

Yield: About 1 1/2 cups syrup

6 lemons
2 cups sugar (or honey)
1 cup water

Carefully remove zest from two of the lemons. Combine water, sugar and lemon zest in a saucepan and bring to a boil. Lower heat and simmer together for 10 minutes. Cool to room temperature. Meanwhile juice the six lemons (you should have about 1 cup of juice). Add to cooled syrup. Strain into a covered jar and store in refrigerator.

To serve put two tablespoons of syrup in a glass add ice cubes and fill with cold water. Stir well.

Lily Soup

Well, that may be stretching definitions a bit, but onions and garlic are somewhat distant relations to the flowering lilies in our summer gardens. Along with chives, shallots, and leeks, they are all members of the allium family. This soup is much milder in flavor than you might expect from reading the ingredients. It is light enough to be used as a first course.

Yield: 6 servings

1/2 cup butter/margarine
4 large yellow onions chopped
4 shallots minced
3 leeks chopped
4 garlic cloves minced
6 cups chicken broth
1 cup cream
2 tbsp cornstarch
2 tbsp water
4 tbsp chopped chives or green onions

Melt butter/margarine in a heavy pan and add chopped onions, shallots, leeks and garlic. Keeping heat low, saute gently until onions are soft and golden (be sure not to rush this step or garlic will turn bitter). Add chicken broth and bring to a boil, reduce heat and simmer for 45 minutes. Remove from heat and cool slightly. Puree mixture in blender or food processor until smooth. Return to saucepan and add cream. Heat to simmer (about 200 degrees Fahrenheit) but do not allow to boil. Taste and add salt if needed. Combine cornstarch and water and add to soup. Stir until slightly thickened. Pour into bowls and garnish with chopped chives or green onions.

Maraschino Cherries

Truly, these are not hard to make… and they look beautiful. You'll find them to be a little larger and juicier than the ones you buy in those little bottles at the store. A jar of Maraschino Cherries makes a nice hospitality gift or a colorful inclusion in an assortment of home-made preserves and pickles as a special present for someone.

Making Maraschino Cherries is a two day job, however, so be sure you allow the time you will need.

Yield: About 8 half pints

- **5 pounds of Royal Anne cherries** (Royal Annes are best, but you can also use other firm, light cherries)
- **1 tbsp alum** (pharmacies carry this if you can't find it at your supermarket)
- **4 tbsp salt** (use kosher or pickling salt, not table salt)
- **7 cups sugar**
- **1 ounce red food coloring**
- **1 tsp almond extract**

(See "Canning Using a Boiling Water Bath Process" on page 29 for complete information on how to process Maraschino Cherries for long-term storage.)

Wash and remove the seeds from the cherries. (A cherry pitter is a handy tool to use for this. The pitter presses the seed out without tearing the fruit apart. Cherry pitters are carried by most stores that stock kitchen gadgets.) You should have about 10 cups of pitted cherries when you finish.

Dissolve the alum and the salt in 2 quarts of cold water. Add the cherries and allow to stand for 6 hours. (If the cherries tend to float, weight them down with a bowl.) Drain the cherries and rinse them with cold water.

In a separate large pan, combine the sugar and 2 cups of cold water. Bring to a boil and cook while you stir until the sugar is dissolved. Add the cherries, bring back to a boil and cook for 2 minutes. Remove from the heat. Add the red food coloring and almond extract and allow to stand in a cool place for 24 hours, stirring from time to time.

The next day, bring the cherries back to a boil and cook for an additional 2 minutes. Pour the boiling hot fruit into the prepared half-pint jars and process them for 5 minutes. (See page 29.)

Store in a cool place.

Marshmallows

Why should a cook make marshmallows when they are so easily available? Perhaps the only reason is curiosity, but that is reason enough. It's always satisfying to find that you can make something that you had previously thought was within the capabilities only of "food manufacturers". The kids will probably enjoy participating in this one too.

Incidentally, the "real" marsh mallow (althaea officialis) is an herb related to the familiar garden hollyhock. Its roots were originally involved in making a confection that has developed into the puffy pillow of bland sweetness we know now.

Yield: About 60 marshmallows

1/4 cup powdered sugar
3 tbsp cornstarch
2 cups granulated sugar
3 envelopes unflavored gelatin
1/4 tsp salt
1 cup cold water
1 tsp vanilla extract (a clear vanilla extract will keep the
    final product as white as possible)

Butter a 9x13-inch baking pan. Combine the powdered sugar and cornstarch in a small bowl. Use a third of the mixture to coat the pan and reserve the rest. Shake the powder combination around in the pan so that it adheres to the sides of the pan as well as the bottom.

Combine the sugar, gelatin and salt in a saucepan. Stir in the cold water and allow to rest for 5 minutes until gelatin softens. Place over low heat and, stirring constantly, heat until the sugar has dissolved. (The mixture should not boil.) When the sugar is dissolved, remove from heat and allow to cool to room temperature. Stir in the vanilla extract. Pour the mixture into a large bowl and, using an electric mixer, beat at high speed until it is thickened and will stand in soft peaks (about 10 to 15 minutes of beating).

Pour the mixture into the pan, spreading to make it smooth and even. Dust the top with the second one-third of the powdered sugar-cornstarch mixture. Loosely cover with foil and let it stand at room temperature undisturbed for at lest two hours or overnight. When the block of candy has set up, remove it from the pan and cut into 1-inch squares or whatever other design you choose. (Dip the knife or cutter into cold water to keep from sticking). Sprinkle with remaining powdered sugar-cornstarch. Store the marshmallows at room temperature in an air-tight container and use within 2 months.

May Wine and May Wine Punch

Woodruff is not easily available to purchase but is very easy to grow yourself in a shady spot in your garden or in a container. It is a pretty plant and a good ground cover. The blossoms appear for about two weeks in May, hence the name. It's the perfect reason to invite some friends in to celebrate the beginning of summer!

Yield: About 16 servings of punch

For the May wine:

- **2 Fifths of semi-sweet white wine** (such as sauterne)
- **1 cup woodruff leaves and blossoms** (washed and stems removed)

Early in the day the May wine is to be served, place the woodruff leaves and flowers in a container large enough to hold both fifths of white wine and add the wine. Cover and chill in refrigerator.

For the May Wine Punch:

- **1 cup sliced strawberries**
- **1 orange thinly sliced**
- **1 lemon thinly sliced**
- **1 fifth of Champagne** (Extra dry is best)

Just before serving time, place a block of ice and the fruits in your punch bowl and strain the white wine as your pour it over. Add the champagne. Decorate with the star-like woodruff leaves and its white flowers that have been rinsed off. The punch can also be made without the fruit and poured from a pretty pitcher.

May Wine Jelly

You can capture the lovely aroma and flavor of May wine for use all year when you make this May Wine Jelly.

Yield: About 4 half-pint jars

    2 cups May wine
    3 cups sugar
    2 wide strips of orange zest
    2 tbsp lemon juice
    1/2 6-ounce bottle of liquid pectin
    4 springs of woodruff for decoration
    Paraffin

Mix wine, sugar, orange zest, and lemon juice in large (non-aluminum) pan. Cook over medium heat, stirring constantly until sugar is dissolved. Keep liquid just under true boil and continue to cook and stir for 5 minutes. Remove from heat and discard orange zest. Stir in pectin and mix well. Skim any foam that forms from top of liquid.

Pour into sterile jars and seal with paraffin wax that has been melted according the directions on the paraffin. When slightly cooled, press a woodruff leaf into the soft wax and then top with another thin layer of wax.

Mayonnaise Cake

This is a recipe that surfaces from time to time and has a flurry of popularity. It is one that you often see requests for in newspapers and magazines. For this recipe you must use a regular mayonnaise, a "diet" or "reduced-calorie" mayonnaise will just not do the job because the oil for the cake comes from the oil in the mayonnaise.

Yield: 8-inch square cake
Oven setting: 375 degrees Fahrenheit

- **2 cups cake flour**
- **1 cup sugar**
- **1 1/2 tsp baking powder**
- **1 1/2 tsp baking soda**
- **5 tbsp dry unsweetened cocoa**
- **1 tsp ground cinnamon**
- **1 1/2 cup mayonnaise**
- **1 cups warm water**
- **1 tsp vanilla**
- **Sweetened whipped cream**

Preheat oven to 375 degrees Fahrenheit. Prepare an 8x8-inch cake pan by greasing and dusting well with flour. Set aside.

Combine flour, sugar, baking powder, baking soda, cocoa, and cinnamon in a bowl. In a separate bowl beat together the mayonnaise and water. Slowly add dry ingredients and mix until smooth. Stir in vanilla.

Pour into prepared pan and bake at 375 degrees Fahrenheit for about 35 minutes or until cake pulls away from the sides of the pan slightly. Turn out onto a cooling rack. To serve, top with a dollop of sweetened whipped cream.

Mincemeat (made with meat)

This is the traditional way to make mincemeat. It was originally a method used to preserve meat by using spices which also tended to cover up the slightly "off" flavor and aroma that developed from the spoiling meat. Fortunately, that is one problem that we don't have to worry about anymore, just make up the mixture and freeze until ready to use.

Yield: About 4 quarts of mincemeat (enough for 4 pies)

- **2 pounds lean beef stew meat** (you can also use wild game such as venison)
- **1/2 pound beef suet** (beef fat you buy from the meat department)
- **1/2 pound chopped candied citron** (you can use mixed candied fruits sold for fruitcakes but it wouldn't be quite traditional)
- **3 pounds tart apples** (Granny Smith's are excellent for this)
- **2 pounds brown sugar**
- **4 cups apple juice or cider**
- **1 tbsp salt**
- **1 tbsp ground nutmeg**
- **1 tbsp ground allspice**
- **1 tbsp ground cinnamon**
- **1 tsp ground cloves**
- **1 cup molasses**
- **1 cup corn syrup**
- **2 pounds dried currants**
- **1 pound golden raisins**
- **1 pound seedless raisins**
- **2 cups brandy**

Place the meat in a deep pan and cover with water. Bring to a boil and then reduce the heat. Simmer until the meat is very tender and the water is almost gone. This will take about an hour.

Cool the meat and put it through your food processor or a food grinder. You should have about 4 or 5 cups of ground meat.

Put the suet through the food process or grinder and add to the meat. Do the same with the candied citron. Peel and finely chop the apples and add them to the meat mixture.

In a separate pan, mix the sugar with the apple juice or cider and mix until the sugar is dissolved. Bring to a boil, reduce the heat and simmer for 5 minutes. Add the meat mixture to the syrup and return to a boil. Reduce the heat again and simmer for about 10 minutes more.

Remove from the heat and add the salt, nutmeg, allspice, cinnamon, cloves, molasses, corn syrup, currants, and raisins. Mix well. Mix in the brandy. Cool to room temperature and either use to make pies or ladle into containers and freeze for later use.

Mincemeat (made without meat)

This is more like the mincemeat we have become accustomed to and many people prefer it to the traditional version. Make it up about Halloween to use for Christmas pies and tarts.

Yield: Enough for 2 generously filled pies or a dozen tarts

- 1/2 cup brown sugar
- 2 cups dark raisins
- 2 cups currants
- 1/2 cup chopped nuts (almonds, walnuts, pecans, or hazelnuts)
- 1 cup chopped tart apple
- 1 cup fine dry bread crumbs
- 1 tbsp grated lemon rind
- 1 tbsp lemon juice
- 1 tsp ground allspice
- 1 tsp ground cinnamon
- 1 tsp ground nutmeg
- 1/2 tsp ground cloves
- 1 tsp almond extract
- 1 cup rum or brandy
- Additional liquid: apple juice, sherry, port, or sweet white wine.

Combine all ingredients and mix well. Pour into a covered container and store in the refrigerator for at least a month before using. Stir about once a week. It will keep for several months if refrigerated. Add some extra liquid if it seems dry.

Mocha Cream Tart

This is a rich dessert, there's no other word to describe it... except maybe delicious. Once in a while a real indulgence is called for and if you like the bland-sharp combination of chocolate and coffee, this might be the one you choose.

Yield: 8 servings

For the shell:

> 1/2 cup butter/margarine
> 1/4 cup powdered sugar
> 3 tbsp cornstarch
> 1/2 tsp almond extract
> 2 cups crumbs made from plain chocolate wafers (about 30)

For the filling:

> 1/2 pound large marshmallows (about 30)
> 1/2 cup milk
> 8 ounces semisweet chocolate
> 2 tbsp very strong coffee (make with instant at double strength)
> 1 cup whipping cream
> Chocolate and whipped cream for garnish

To make the shell:

Combine chocolate, crumbs, powdered sugar and cornstarch. Melt the butter/margarine and combine it with the almond extract. Add melted butter/margerine to crumbs combination and mix well. (You'll find the result will resemble mud.) Press the crumbs into the bottom and up the sides of an 9-inch pie pan and put in the refrigerator to firm.

To make the filling:

Put the marshmallows in the top portion of a double boiler and add the milk. Cook over simmering water until the marshmallows melt, stirring occasionally. (This takes a while so be patient.) Allow to cool to room temperature. Melt the chocolate. Whip the cream. When the marshmallow mixture has cooled, add the coffee and then the melted chocolate. Finally, fold in the whipped cream. Gently pour the filling into the prepared shell. Chill at least 1 hour before serving (even longer is better).

Garnish with whipped cream (either whip some more or use some from an aerosol can for a pretty design) and add either chocolate that you have shaved from a square of semisweet chocolate with your vegetable peeler, or use chocolate sprinkles.

Marinated Mushrooms

Marinated mushrooms are a great addition to a collection of hors d'oeuvres for a cocktail party, they also go well as a garnish for a green salad, or simply on their own served with broiled steak.

Yield: You will get about 50 small mushrooms in a pound.

1 pound small mushrooms
1 cup olive oil
1/2 cup water
1/4 cup lemon juice
1/2 tsp dried thyme
1/2 tsp dried rosemary
1/2 tsp dried oregano
2 cloves garlic sliced
10 whole peppercorns
1 tsp salt

Cut stems from mushrooms and use for some other purpose. Clean with brush (or peel if you prefer although some flavor is lost with the peeling).

In a saucepan combine oil, water, lemon juice, thyme, rosemary, oregano, garlic, peppercorns and salt. Bring to a boil, lower heat and simmer for 15 minutes. Strain into a small bowl and discard spices. Return liquid to pan, add mushrooms and quickly bring to a boil. Reduce heat and simmer, uncovered for 5 minutes.

Pour mushrooms and marinade into a jar with a cover and chill in refrigerator for a day or two before serving.

To serve, remove from refrigerator and drain off marinade at least a half hour before serving. They taste better at room temperature.

Dijon-style Mustard

Of course you can make your own Dijon-style mustard... and the best part is that you can adjust the seasonings to your particular pleasure. It's not hard to do... and also makes a nice gift.

Yield: About 1 1/2 cups

1 large onion
3 cloves of garlic
2 cups dry white wine
4 ounces of dry mustard
4 tbsp honey
1 tbsp mild oil (such as sunflower or corn)
2 tsp salt

Peal and finely chop the onion. Peel and mince the garlic (or put through a garlic press). Combine the onion and garlic with the wine in a saucepan. Bring to a boil and then reduce the heat and simmer for 10 minutes. Remove from the heat and cool slightly. Pour through a strainer and discard the onion and garlic.

Add the dry mustard to the flavored wine to make a paste. Add the honey, oil, and salt and mix well. Return the mixture to the saucepan and cook over low heat until it thickens while you stir constantly. (Since there are no thickening agents used, you will be thickening it by evaporating the liquid away.)

Cool to room temperature and then stir well and store in a covered jar in the refrigerator.

Horseradish Mustard

Homemade mustards are fun to make, a pleasure to use, and always a welcome gift. There are recipes for a wide variety of mustards, but this one is particularly versatile.

Yield: About 1 cup of prepared mustard

1 cup dry mustard
3/4 cup white wine vinegar (tarragon vinegar is nice to use)
1/4 cup water
1/3 cup sugar
1 tsp onion powder
1 tsp caraway seeds
2 eggs, beaten
1/4 cup olive oil
1 tbsp fresh horseradish

Combine mustard, vinegar, water, sugar, onion powder and caraway seeds and let stand for several hours at room temperature. (If you have a mortar and pestle, crush the seeds slightly.)

Mix eggs and olive oil together and add to mustard mixture. In a small pan over low-to-medium heat cook the mixture slowly, stirring constantly until it thickens (about 15 minutes). Remove from heat and add horseradish and stir in well. Pour into a covered container and store in refrigerator.

Wait at least a day before using to let the flavors blend. Because of the eggs in the recipe, this mustard must be stored in the refrigerator to prevent spoilage.

Sweet-and-Hot Mustard

This simple-to-make mustard is one that you will particularly like with ham. It also makes a nice gift, just put it in a pretty jar (but be sure to remind your gift recipient that it should be stored in the refrigerator).

Yield: About 2 cups

4 ounces dry mustard
1 cup vinegar
3 eggs
1 cup sugar

Combine dry mustard and vinegar in a small bowl with a cover. Cover and refrigerate overnight.

Beat eggs and sugar until well blended. Add to mustard mixture and pour into the top section of a double boiler. Keep water in lower section just at simmer temperature. Cook, stirring constantly, until thickened and smooth (about 7-8 minutes). Pour into jar with a tight lid and store in refrigerator. This is best if you allow it to mellow for a day or two before using.

Nasturtium "Capers"

True capers are the unopened flower buds of a spiny training shrub that grows in the Mediterranean area, Capparis spinosa. The buds are dried and then pickled in vinegar and spices. Capers are lovely to use but expensive. Nasturtium flowers produce small green seed pods that can be pickled to produce a similar, although certainly not identical, product.

Yield: 2 cups "capers"

2 cup immature (green) **nasturtium seeds**
12 tbsp salt
2 quarts water
1/2 tsp mustard seed
1/2 tsp dill seed
1 cup cider vinegar
1 tsp salt
1 tsp peppercorns
1 clove garlic, sliced

(See "Canning Using a Boiling Water Bath Process" on page 29 for complete information on how to process the Nasturtium Capers for long-term storage.)

Pick nasturtium seeds just after the blossoms drop and before the seed dries out. In a glass bowl, dissolve 6 tbsp salt in 1 quart of water. Add nasturtium seeds and soak overnight. Drain the next day and repeat the process. On the third day drain then divide the seeds between the two half-pint jars.

In a saucepan, combine vinegar, 1 tsp salt, dill seed, mustard seed, peppercorns and garlic bring to a boil. Strain liquid over nasturtium seeds. Cap with new lids and tighten rings. Process in boiling water bath to cover for 15 minutes. (See page 29.)

Cool and store in a cool place. (Alternately, after pouring strained liquid over the seeds, you may cover and store in refrigerator for up to a month.)

Nasturtium Salad

Although we tend to think of nasturtiums as colorful additions to our summer gardens (that sometimes get out of hand and seem to take over everything!), both flowers and leaves are quite edible and make an interesting addition to your summer cooking. Try a small number of the leaves in any green salad, they are a little peppery and definitely brighten up milder greens. This salad is based on cucumbers which are be a bit bland and can benefit from the flavor of the nasturtiums.

Yield: 6 servings

    4 cucumbers*
    8-10 nasturtium leaves**
    1/2 cup chopped green onions (including green tops)
    1/4 cup chopped fresh parsley
    1/4 cup olive oil
    1/4 cup other salad oil (sunflower or corn are fine)
    1/4 cup white wine vinegar
    1/4 cup sugar
    2-3 drops of hot pepper sauce (such as *Tabasco*)
    8-10 nasturtium flowers

*Some people either don't like or can't eat cucumbers, consider using zucchini as a substitute.

**Do not eat nasturtium leaves or flowers if you use insecticides in your planting area.

Peel the cucumbers, cut them in half lengthwise and remove the seeds. Shred them into longish strands using a grater or food processor.

Wash the nasturtium leaves very well and cut into strips. Add the chopped green onion, nasturtium leaf strips, and chopped parsley to the shredded cucumber.

Mix the oils, vinegar, sugar and pepper sauce together and pour over the vegetables. Toss lightly together and turn out into a serving bowl and garnish with the nasturtium blossoms (which you have washed carefully).

Honey-glazed Nuts

These nuts should be eaten within a week. Hard to believe they could even last that long because they are so good! If you would like something similar that is not deep fried, try the recipe for Sugar and Spice Glazed Nuts that follows.

Yield: About 4 cups of coated nuts

3 cups water
1 cup honey
1 pound shelled unsalted nuts (almonds, peanuts,
cashews, walnuts, or pecans)
1/2 cup white sugar
2 cups vegetable oil

Combine water and honey in a large pan and bring to a boil. Add nuts and simmer for 5 minutes. Drain off liquid but leave nuts in pan. Add sugar and toss the nuts to coat them completely with sugar.

Remove from pan and place on waxed paper so they do not touch each other.

Heat oil in deep fryer or other deep pan to 350 degrees Fahrenheit. Depending on the size of your container put in only the amount of nuts that can fry without sticking together. Fry until just golden brown (until sugar is slightly caramelized but not browned or it will taste bitter). Using a slotted spoon, remove and drain on paper towels.

Continue until all the nuts are glazed. Let the nuts cool and dry. Store at room temperature.

Sugar-and-Spice Glazed Nuts

This recipe glazes the nuts in the oven rather than in the deep fryer. The eggs whites, however, help to make the glaze quite crisp and the spices also add additional flavor. These make a nice holiday gift.

Yield: 1/2 pound of glazed nuts
Oven setting: 250 degrees Fahrenheit

  1 cup sugar
  1/2 cup cornstarch
  1/4 tsp salt
  3 tsp ground cinnamon
  1 tsp ground allspice
  1 tsp ground nutmeg
  2 egg whites
  3 tbsp water
  1/2 pound shelled unsalted nut halves

Combine the sugar, cornstarch, salt, cinnamon, allspice and nutmeg in a small bowl.

In a separate bowl beat the egg whites and water together until they are foamy.

Drop the nut halves into the egg mixture. Stir the nuts so that they are well coated with the egg whites. With a slotted spoon remove a few nuts at a time and drop them into the dry ingredients. Toss to coat well with the sugar-and-spice mixture and then place on a cookie sheet. (They should not touch each other.)

Bake at 250 degrees Fahrenheit for 1 hour. The nuts should be crisp but not browned. Cool to room temperature and then store in an air-tight container.

Olive Bread

If you enjoy making breads, you will want to try this one. When the loaves are cut, rounds of black and stuffed olives appear. It is very nice to serve with barbecued meats. A good bread to take for a pot-luck contribution.

Yield: 2 or 3 large loaves
Oven setting: 325 degrees Fahrenheit

 1 pkg dry yeast
 3/4 cup warm (100 degree Fahrenheit) water
 1/2 cup soft butter/margarine
 1/4 cup sugar
 2 tsp salt
 4 large eggs
 5 cups white flour (bread flour is best)
 1 1/2 cups stuffed green olives
 1 1/2 cups pitted medium black olives
 1 egg yolk mixed with 1 tbsp water

In a small bowl combine the yeast and warm water, mix and allow to stand for 5 minutes. Cream together butter/margarine, sugar, and salt until well blended.

Add eggs one at a time and blend well after each one. Stir in the yeast/water mixture. Stir in about 4 cups of the flour and mix well. Knead using the dough hook on your mixer, in your food processor, or by hand for about 10 minutes adding the remaining cup of flour. Dough should be smooth and pliable.

Place in a oiled bowl, then rotate so that oiled side of dough is up, cover with plastic wrap and allow to raise in a warm place until the dough is doubled in size (about 90 minutes).

Drain olives well and roll them in a paper towel to absorb excess liquid. (If you like, you can chop the olives coarsely before blotting.)

Turn the dough out onto a floured board and divide it into three parts. Roll each part out to a rough rectangle about 10" by 12". Scatter 1/2 cup of each of the olive types on each third of the dough. Pressing tightly together as you roll, roll the dough so that you have a loaf about 12 inches long when you finish. Pinch to seal and place with seam down on a cookie sheet. Cover with plastic wrap and let raise for an additional 30 minutes.

Uncover carefully and gently brush with egg yolk/water mixture. (Use your fingers to spread the egg yolk evenly over the loaves.) Bake in a 325 degree oven until golden (about 45 minutes). Cool on a rack for at least 10 minutes before cutting. (Baked loaves freeze well.)

Spiced Onion Rings

These spicy onion pickles are easy to make and will be popular with anyone who likes onions. They are great on a hamburger and also a nice accompaniment for baked beans.

Yield: About 6 pints

6 large red onions
6 cinnamon sticks
2 tsp whole cloves
1 tsp whole peppercorns
5 cups white vinegar
2 1/2 cups water
2 cups sugar
2 tsp salt

(See "Canning Using a Boiling Water Bath Process" on page 29 for complete information on how to process the Spiced Onion Rings for long-term storage.)

Slice onion into thin slices then separate slices into rings. Break up cinnamon sticks and mix with cloves and peppercorns. Put about 2 inches of onion rings into each of 6 sterilized pint containers. Sprinkle with spices. Repeat until onion is used, ending with a layer of onions.

Combine vinegar, water, sugar, and salt and bring to a boil Pour over onions and spices to within 1/4 inch of rim of bottle. Process for 15 minutes. (See page 29.) Store in a cool place.

This recipe may also be made in smaller batches and kept in the refrigerator. If prepared this way, allow at least a day after making for the flavors to blend before serving.

Crisp Onions

These are a lot like French fried onion rings, but not identical. Instead of the huge, thick rings, the onions are cut very thin. The result is crispy and flavorful. They are delicious with burgers or other sandwiches... also good sprinkled on top of soup. You can also make them in advance and keep in the freezer (to reheat, spread out on a cookie sheet and heat in a 350 degree oven until warmed through).

Yield: 6-10 servings depending on how you use them

1 1/2 pounds yellow onions
1/2 cup all-purpose flour
Oil for frying
Salt

Peel the onions and cut into very thin slices. Separate the slices into rings. Put the flour into a plastic bag, add a portion of the rings and shake to coat with flour. Continue until all of the rings are coated.

Using a deep fat fryer or a deep saucepan, bring at least 2 inches of oil up to 300 degrees Fahrenheit, you'll need a deep fat thermometer for this. If you maintain the cooking temperature of the oil they will not be greasy.

Cook about a fourth of the onions at a time, turning so they become golden brown on all sides. Be sure to regulate the heat so that you maintain temperature between 275 and 300 degrees.

When the onions are light brown, remove them from the oil with a slotted spoon and drain on paper towels. Sprinkle lightly with salt. Eat right away (they're hard to resist), or store in the refrigerator for a day or two, or freeze (for up to 4 weeks).

Orange Cake

If you cook for someone who has to control saturated fats, but still likes a piece of cake from time to time, here is something you can serve. Because it uses only egg whites and oil rather than shortening or butter, it is cholesterol-free... and tastes good too! A pleasant, light cake.

Yield: 5x8-inch loaf (about 8 servings)
Oven setting: 350 degrees Fahrenheit

> **4 egg whites**
> **1 1/2 cups cake flour**
> **1 cup sugar**
> **2 tsp baking powder**
> **1/4 tsp salt**
> **1/2 cup mild oil** (corn or sunflower)
> **1/2 cup orange juice**
> **2 tsp grated orange zest**

Prepare a 5x8-inch loaf pan by greasing and dusting with flour. Set aside.

Beat the egg whites until stiff enough to leave a firm peak when the beater is removed.

With your electric mixer, mix together the flour, sugar, baking powder and salt. In a separate bowl blend oil, orange juice, and grated orange zest. Pour the oil-juice mixture into the dry ingredients and mix until smooth.

Gently fold in the egg whites. Be sure to use a U-shaped motion so that you capture as much of the egg white volume as possible. Be sure that all of the egg whites are smoothly incorporated.

Carefully pour into the prepared pan and bake at 350 degrees for about 1 hour or until the cake pulls away from the sides of the pan slightly. Cool in the pan for 10 minutes and then turn out onto a cooling rack.

Orange Egg Nog Shake

Kids love this, and with the orange juice, milk, egg combination, it is pretty good for them too. The flavor is a bit reminiscent of the Orange Julius *brand drinks that everyone seems to like.*

Yield: About 6 cups

1 6-ounce can frozen orange juice undiluted
1 cup milk
1 cup cold water
1/2 cup sugar
1 tsp vanilla extract
10-12 ice cubes

Mix all ingredients except ice cubes. Pour half into blender container and add 5-6 ice cubes. Cover and blend until smooth (about 30 seconds or so). Repeat with remaining mixture and ice.

Head-start Pastrami

This recipe does not make true pastrami, but the flavor comes very close and it is do-able in your own kitchen. Slice into very thin slices for sandwiches or buffet.

Yield: 10 to 12 servings
Oven setting: 350 degrees Fahrenheit

> **6 pound piece of corned beef**
> **Water**
> **6 cloves of garlic, crushed**
> **2 tbsp pickling spice**
> **3 tbsp coarsely cracked peppercorns**
> **1 tsp ground allspice**
> **1 tsp ground mace**
> **1 tsp paprika**

Trim any visible fat from corned beef. Place the meat in a baking pan that has a tight lid and is at least 2 inches deep. Add garlic and pickling spice and enough water to cover the meat. Cover pan. Bake at 350 for 3 hours until meat is tender. (You will be returning the meat to the oven so you may want to leave the oven turned on.) Refrigerate the meat and allow it to cool in the liquid until it is cool enough to handle. Drain and discard the water and seasonings. While the meat is cooling, combine pepper, allspice, mace, and paprika. Rub the combined spices over all sides. Return to the oven and bake, uncovered now, for about 30 minutes more or until lightly browned.

The meat can be served with hot or cold but let it rest about 20 minutes before trying to slice. It is best to cut it diagonally across the grain of the meat.

Curried Pea Soup

This is particularly nice to serve in the summer as a cold soup because it makes you feel cooler just to look at it. But it is equally good as a hot soup and light enough that you can start a meal with a small bowl of it without spoiling interest in what is yet to come.

Yield: 4 servings

    1 cup diced peeled potatoes
    2 cups chicken broth
    1 cup frozen peas
    1/4 cup chopped green onions (with tops)
    1/2 tsp curry powder (more or less to taste)
    1/2 tsp salt
    1 cup half-and-half (light cream)
    Paprika

Cook potatoes in chicken broth until tender. Add frozen peas and simmer for 5 minutes.

Pour mixture into blender or food processor and puree. Add curry powder, salt and half-and-half.

Soup may be heated or served cold. Garnish with paprika, or a spoonful of finely chopped peanuts, or some chopped chives.

Cream of Peanut Soup

Admittedly this sounds a little strange, but until you have tried it, reserve judgment. It will be especially popular with anyone who enjoys peanut butter, and even those who wouldn't ever look at a classic peanut butter-and-jelly sandwich will find this flavor hard to criticize.

Yield: 6 servings

1/3 cup butter/margarine
1 medium onion finely chopped
3/4 cup finely chopped celery
3 tbsp all purpose flour
3 cups chicken broth
1 1/2 cups milk
1 cup half-and-half (light cream)
1 cup creamy-style peanut butter
Pepper to taste
Finely chopped peanuts

Melt butter/margarine and saute onion and celery until they are tender. Add flour, stirring constantly, the gradually add chicken broth. Using a whisk, stir until smooth and it comes to a boil. Remove from heat and add milk and half-and-half.

Strain soup and discard onion and celery. Add peanut butter and mix well. Return to heat and warm to serving temperature. Taste and add pepper.

Serve in bowls and garnish with a sprinkle of chopped peanuts.

Peanut Butter Waffles

Along with chocolate, peanut butter has to be one of mankind's favorite foods. In the United States something like 700 million pounds of peanut butter are sold every year! However, even people who are not real fans of peanut butter will like this tasty waffle variation for a change of pace. The waffles are particularly good when served with honey. Feel free to add more chopped peanuts if you like more crunch.

Yield: 4 generous servings

  1/2 cup chunky peanut butter
  1/4 cup softened butter/margarine
  1/4 cup sugar
  2 eggs
  2 cups milk
  1 3/4 cups cake flour
  1 tbsp baking powder
  1/2 tsp salt
  1/4 cup chopped peanuts

Heat the waffle iron. Cream the peanut butter and softened butter/margarine together. Separate the eggs. Add egg yolks and milk to peanut butter mixture and mix well. Combine flour, baking powder and salt. Beat egg whites until they hold a firm peak. Add dry ingredients and chopped peanuts to batter. Fold in the egg whites.

Bake until golden brown in the preheated waffle iron.

Peanut Honey Bread

One more recipe for peanut fans... this is a quick bread to serve as a snack bread or to include in the brown-bag lunches you prepare. Use your favorite brand of honey-roasted peanut or make your own using the recipe on page 117.

Yield: 1 loaf
Oven setting: 350 degrees Fahrenheit

> **2 cups flour**
> **2 tsp baking powder**
> **1/2 tsp salt**
> **1 cup chunky peanut butter**
> **1 egg**
> **2 tbsp butter/margarine**
> **1/4 cup honey**
> **1 cup milk**
> **1/2 to 1 cup chopped honey-roasted peanuts**

Mix flour, baking powder and salt together. Using a pastry blender or mixer, cut in the peanut butter. Beat egg lightly and melt the butter/margarine. Mix egg, butter/margarine, honey and milk together and stir into first mixture. Fold in the chopped peanuts. Pour into a well-greased 9x5-inch loaf pan and bake at 350 degrees Fahrenheit for about an hour or until cake tester comes out clean. Cool in pan for 5 minutes and then turn out onto cooling rack. Allow to cool completely before cutting.

Pear and Almond Tart

This is an elegant dessert to serve either to end a dinner party or for a dessert-and-coffee evening with friends. It takes a bit of time to prepare, but it is not really difficult. It is nice to have a tart pan with a removable bottom for this recipe, but if you don't, don't worry, it will taste just as good if you make it in a large pie pan.

Yield: 8 servings at least... maybe even 10
Oven setting: 300 degrees Fahrenheit (for the shell)

For the shell:

> 1 1/2 cups flour
> 1/3 cup sugar
> 2 tsp finely grated lemon peel
> 1/2 cup cold butter/margarine
> 1 egg yolk

For the filling:

> 1/3 cup powdered sugar
> 1 tsp finely grated lemon peel
> 2 tsp strained fresh lemon juice
> 1/2 tsp vanilla extract
> 1/2 tsp almond extract
> 3 ounces of cream cheese at room temperature
> 1 cup whipping cream
> 8 small cooked pear halves (usually a 28-ounce can)
> 1/2 cup apple jelly
> 1/2 cup sliced almonds

To make the shell:

Combine the flour, sugar, and lemon peel in a small bowl and cut in the butter/margarine using a pastry blender. Work the mixture until it is like coarse cornmeal and there are no lumps of butter/margarine left.

Add the egg yolk and work it in with your hands until it is well distributed and the dough will make a ball. Press the dough into an 11-inch tart pan, or 10-inch spring-form pan. (You can use a large pie pan to make the tart. If you do you will probably have dough left over.) With a fork, prick the bottom of the shell in several places.

Place in a 300 degree oven and bake for 30 minutes until golden brown. Cool to room temperature.

To make the tart:

Combine the powdered sugar, lemon peel, lemon juice, and almond and vanilla extracts.

In a small bowl, using an electric hand-mixer, beat the cream cheese until smooth and then slowly add the whipping cream. Mix in the powdered sugar combination and continue to beat until the mixture is about like whipped cream. Carefully ladle the mixture into the cooled shell.

Drain the pears. Trim one into a circular shape to put in the center of the tart and then arrange the other halves around it. Press the pear pieces gently into the filling.

Put the apple jelly in a small pan and melt it over low heat. Pour the melted jelly over the pears and smooth to make a shiny surface. Sprinkle the almond slices around the edge or scatter across the entire surface, whichever you prefer.

Chill for at least 1 hour before serving. If you make this up early in the day, cover lightly with foil but be careful not to let the foil rest on the surface or the smoothness of the jelly will be disturbed.

Pimentos

Tiny jars of pimentos are quite expensive to buy. Sweet red bell peppers can easily be made into pimentos that you can have on hand to use all the time at minimal cost. You will find many ways of using them in salads, soups, and casseroles where their bright red color adds an appetizing contrast.

Yield: About 1 cup pimentos

4 sweet red bell peppers
Boiling water
1 cup cider vinegar
1 cup water
1/2 cup sugar
1 tsp salt
2 tsp olive oil

Clean peppers and remove stem, seeds, and white pith. Cut into strips. Cover with boiling water and allow to stand for 5 minutes. Drain. While peppers are steeping, bring to a boil vinegar, water, sugar and salt and simmer for 5 minutes.

Place pepper strips in a sterilized quart bottle and pour the vinegar mixture over them. Cover and store in the refrigerator. Peppers should marinate for about two weeks before you use them.

The pimentos will keep for several weeks in the refrigerator but for longer storage, if you use them only occasionally, divide among small containers and freeze. This will make about 3-4 cups of pimento strips.

Pirozhki

Filled pastries are found all over the world. Baking some meat and vegetables and a bit of sauce in a piece of dough makes a compact lunch to carry to field or factory. Filled baked pastries are still easy-to make, easy-to-carry, and easy-to-eat, and consequently still popular. These particular filled pastry snacks are a culinary contribution from Russia. Serve diminutive versions as appetizers and full-grown size for a main dish... a good take-away for picnics too.

Yield: 30 to 36 pastries
Oven setting: 400 degrees Fahrenheit

For the filling:

   1/2 **ground lean** (or extra lean) **ground beef**
   1/2 **cup very finely chopped onion**
   1 **very finely chopped hard-cooked egg**
   1/2 **tsp dried thyme**
   1/2 **tsp salt**
   1/4 **tsp pepper**

To make the filling:

Cook ground beef until lightly browned and transfer to a small mixing bowl. Cook chopped onion until golden and combine with meat. Mix in chopped hard-cooked egg, thyme, salt, and pepper.

For the pastry:

   1 1/2 **cups flour**
   3 **ounces cream cheese**
   1/2 **cup cold butter/margarine**

To make the pastry:

Place flour in mixing bowl and add cream cheese and butter/margarine. Combine by cutting with a pastry blender until it looks like fine crumbs. Form the dough into a ball and chill for 30 minutes. Cut ball in half and roll out to about 1/4 inch thickness.

(You can use your favorite pie crust recipe if you like, but this pastry made with cream cheese is one more commonly used to make piroshki.)

Cut into circles (2 1/2 to 3 inches in diameter is best for appetizers, larger if you are going to use as a main dish). For the smaller size, place about 1 tsp of the meat filling one side of each, add more for a larger serving. Moisten around the entire edge of a circle and fold it over. Press well to seal. Do the same with each circle. And repeat the rolling, cutting, filling and sealing with the remaining portion of the dough.

Bake on ungreased baking sheet at 400 for 12-15 minutes or until golden brown.

Pistachio Cheese Spread

This is a spread with some crunch. If you can't find pistachios, you can also use chopped blanched almonds, the flavor will be different but the texture will be similar.

Yield: About 1 1/2 cups of spread

8 ounces cream cheese
1 cup cream
1 green onion minced
1 tbsp brandy
1/2 cup chopped pistachio nuts
1/2 tsp salt

Allow cream cheese to soften. Whip cream until stiff. Add green onion, brandy, chopped pistachios, and salt. Beat cheese until soft enough to fold in the whipped cream mixture. Chill. Mound to serve. Garnish with a few chopped pistachios.

Pomander Ball

Pomander balls are a gift from the 16th century to us. Originally designed to be held to the nose to cover unpleasant odors, they gradually came to be associated with health-preserving properties. The pomander often was contained in a lovely filigree metal ball and worn from the waist on a chain. Pomanders were commonly presented as New Year's Day gifts to close friends in those times.

These days pomanders make a nice addition to your closet or clothing storage drawers, and are still a welcome home-made gift.

Fruit: oranges, apples, quinces, lemons, or limes
Whole cloves to cover (allow about 1/4 pound per pomander ball)
1/3 cup powdered orris root (available from pharmacies)
1/3 cup ground allspice
1/4 cup ground cinnamon
1/8 cup ground cloves
1/8 cup ground nutmeg
1 tbsp ground ginger

The fruit should be as perfectly shaped as possible and have a firm skin. Stud the surface evenly and completely with whole cloves (the peel should be hardly visible). Mix powdered orris root and spices in a large bowl. Roll the clove-studded fruit in the powder and press it well into the clove covering. Leave the pomander ball in the bowl with the powdered mixture and turn it daily. The pulp will dry slowly and when the process in finished the ball will be light feeling and very aromatic.

Tie the ball with bright ribbons for hanging and decoration.

Caramelized Popcorn

Remember those boxes of popcorn-nut candy with the funny looking kid in a sailor suit on the front... and the "prize"? Well, this is the closest you'll come to capturing that nostalgic flavor. It's fun to make too. (But you have to add your own "prize"!)

Yield: A lot... enough for probably 6 people
Oven setting: 250 degrees Fahrenheit

   1/2 cup oil
   2/3 cup popcorn kernels (unpopped)
   1 1/2 cups salted dry roasted peanuts
   1/2 cup butter/margarine
   1/4 cup dark molasses
   1/2 cup honey
   1/4 cup brown sugar
   1/4 tsp baking soda
   1 tsp vanilla extract

Pop the corn in the oil. You should have about 12 cups of popped corn when you finish. Put the popped corn (with any unpopped kernels removed) into a large bowl and add the peanuts. Mix together.

Melt the butter/margarine in a small saucepan. Add the molasses, honey, and brown sugar. Stir to dissolve the brown sugar and heat until bubbles appear around the edge of the pan. Remove from heat and add the baking soda and vanilla. Immediately pour over the popcorn and nuts. Mix with two large spoons so that everything is coated with the syrup.

Spread the mixture out on two cookie sheets and bake at 250 for 40 minutes. (It's a good idea to turn the pans once during the baking time.) The candy should be a golden brown in color.

Cool completely. Serve at once or store in an airtight container. It will keep for about a week in the unlikely event that it is not eaten immediately.

Barbecued Pork Spareribs

When you think of barbecuing spareribs, New Zealand is not a place that immediately springs to mind. Nevertheless, this unusual barbecued spareribs recipe comes from there. It is different from most in that the ribs are not covered with a thick barbecue sauce but rather are marinated and cooked, the result being a very flavorful, but not sticky meat dish.

Incidentally, if you are concerned about salt intake, you may cut back on the soy sauce or leave it out completely.

Yield: 4 servings

    1 8-ounce can of tomato sauce
    1 can of condensed beef consomme
    1/3 cup soy sauce
    1 cup brown sugar
    1/3 cup sherry
    1/2 cup finely chopped green pepper
    1/2 cup finely chopped onion
    1/2 cup finely chopped celery
    1 clove of garlic, minced
    1 tsp dried rosemary
    1 tsp dried oregano
    1 tsp dried basil
    1 dried bay leaf
    (1/2 tsp liquid smoke seasoning if you like)
    4 pounds of country ribs (as meaty as possible)

Combine tomato sauce, consomme, soy sauce, brown sugar, sherry, green pepper, onion, celery, garlic, rosemary, oregano, basil and the bay leaf to make a marinade. (Liquid smoke may be added to the marinade if you wish.)

Place the ribs in a glass dish large enough to hold them without crowding. Pour the marinade over the meat and allow it to repose in the liquid for at least 24 hours... even longer is better, up to about 48 hours.

To cook indoors, arrange the ribs on your broiler and place them about 6 inches from the heat. Broil for 45-60 minutes, turning from time to time until they are thoroughly done.

The ribs can also be cooked outdoors over a barbecue.

Cowboy Potatoes

Where this name came from is a puzzle. It's hard to imagine chuck-wagon chefs having the facilities to make them up for the boys at the end of the day... on the other hand, perhaps these came from the times the cowboys spent their nights in the bunkhouse instead of on the trail and their dinner was prepared in a wood-burning stove. Whatever the case, it's a good way to fix potatoes... crisp as French fries without the fat.

Yield: 6 Servings
Oven setting: 450 degrees Fahrenheit

1 1/2 pound new potatoes
1/4 cup oil
1 tsp salt
1/2 tsp ground pepper

Scrub the potatoes (but don't peel them) and cut them into 1/2 inch dice. Heat the oil in a heavy skillet and add the potatoes. Season with salt and pepper and mix until the potatoes are coated with the hot oil.

Turn the warmed potatoes out onto a cookie sheet that you have sprayed with vegetable oil spray. Try to keep the pieces of potato somewhat separated from each other. Place the pan in the heated oven and cook for about 45 minutes, stirring at least every 15 minutes. The potatoes will brown as they cook and the result will be crispy little diced potatoes.

Prawns in Beer

Anyone who likes shrimp will like this dish... what more is there to say!

Yield: 4 generous servings

To cook the prawns:

> **1 12 ounce can of beer**
> **2 tsp salt**
> **1 tbsp whole peppercorns**
> **1 small dry red pepper**
> **1 tsp onion powder**
> **1 tsp garlic powder**
> **1 tsp dry mustard**
> **2 pounds large** (or medium) **raw prawns** (weight with shells)

Combine beer, salt, peppercorns, dry red pepper, onion powder, garlic powder, and dry mustard and cook for 20 minutes. While the marinade is cooking, remove shells and "veins" from prawns but leave tail attached. Add the shrimp to the mixture and cook 20 minutes more while you prepare the dip.

To make the zesty cream cheese dipping sauce:

> **3 ounces cream cheese**
> **1 tsp creamy horseradish**
> **1 tbsp grated onion**
> **1/4 tsp pepper sauce**
> **Salt to taste**
> **Half-and-half** (light cream)

Soften cream cheese and mix in horseradish, grated onion, pepper sauce and salt to taste. Add half-and-half to thin to dipping consistency.

To serve:
On individual serving plates, arrange prawns around a small bowl of sauce for dipping.

Soft Rye Pretzels

These big pretzels are an excellent snack food... low in both fat and sugar. The pretzels are a little on the salty side though, so if salt intake is a consideration, you might want to pass them by.

In addition to being good on their own, the pretzels also go well with a soup or salad for a light lunch or supper too.

Yield: About 16-18 pretzels
Oven setting: 400 degrees Fahrenheit

1 pkg dry yeast (or 1 scant tbsp)
1/2 cup warm water (90-100 degrees Fahrenheit)
2 cups milk
1/4 cup sugar
1 tsp salt
1/4 cup mild oil
2 tsp caraway seeds
3 cups rye flour
3 cups bread flour (all-purpose flour can be used)
2 tbsp salt in about 2 quarts of boiling water
1 egg white
(Coarse salt)

Dissolve the yeast in the warm water and allow to rest for 5 minutes. Warm the milk to lukewarm and place it in a large bowl with the sugar, 1 tsp of the salt, mild oil, and caraway seeds. Mix well. Add the rye flour and mix. Add the white flour until the dough will absorb no more and then turn out onto a floured board and knead in the rest of the white flour. Continue to knead for about 10 minutes until the dough is smooth and elastic. (If using a dough hook on mixer or food processor, knead for about 10 minutes.)

Cover and allow to raise in a warm place until doubled (about 1 hour.) Punch the dough down and immediately roll it out to form a rectangle (about 10x15 inches). Cut the dough into long strips and form into the "knot" that is the traditional pretzel shape. Place on a tray or cookie sheet and allow to raise for 30 minutes.

Bring the water to a boil and add the 2 tbsp salt. When the pretzels have raised, drop them one at a time into the boiling water. Leave them there for only about 5 seconds (just to "set" the outside of the dough) and then lift out using a slotted spoon and drain on a cooling rack.

When all have been "par boiled", arrange them on a greased cooking sheet, allow about 1 inch between them. Brush with lightly beaten egg white (and lightly sprinkle with coarse salt if you wish). Bake at 400 for about 20 minutes, or until golden brown. Serve immediately or cool to room temperature and store in air-tight bags.

Pudding Mix

Mixes are a great time saver for busy cooks. There are some that, because they are so versatile, are more valuable than others and this basic pudding mix falls into that category. No, it isn't "instant" but it is quick, and in addition to that, you know exactly what is in it... no fillers, no additives, just simple, nutritious ingredients.

Yield: About 4 cups of pudding mix

To prepare mix:

> **2 cups dry nonfat milk**
> **1 cup sugar**
> **1 cup flour**
> **1 tsp salt**

Mix all ingredients together. Store in jar with tight lid and use within about three months.

To make Vanilla Pudding:

> **1 cup pudding mix**
> **2 cups warm water**
> **1 tbsp butter/margarine**
> **1 slightly beaten egg**
> **1 tsp vanilla extract**

In the top of a double boiler, mix 1 cup pudding mix with two cups warm water. Put over boiling water and cook until thickened stirring constantly. Reduce heat to low under the boiling water. Cover the upper part of the pan and continue cooking for about 10 minutes (stir once or twice during this time). Add butter/margarine and stir. Remove from heat. Slowly, in a thin stream, pour half of hot mixture into beaten egg and mix well. Pour egg mixture back into remaining hot pudding mixture, and replace top of double boiler on the bottom section holding boiling water and cook for another minute.

Cool slightly, stir once or twice, then put plastic wrap down on surface of pudding and chill. Makes 4 servings. (Be sure to use double boiler to cook because cooking over direct heat will cause the pudding to be gummy and not smooth.)

Variations Using Pudding Mix:

To make Butterscotch Pudding Mix:
Substitute brown sugar for white. Otherwise follow directions above.

To make Chocolate Pudding Mix:
Add 3 tbsp cocoa powder to ingredients for vanilla pudding and make according to directions above.

To make Rice Pudding using Pudding Mix:
Mix 2 cups cooked rice into prepared vanilla pudding. Add some raisins if your like. Dust top with ground nutmeg (freshly grated is best).

To make Peanut Butter Pudding using Pudding Mix:
Mix 1/3 cup peanut butter and 1/4 cup chopped peanuts into hot prepared vanilla pudding (you can add some chocolate chips to this when it has cooled).

To make Coconut, Banana, or other fruit pudding using Pudding Mix:
Add 1/2 to 1 cup fruit to prepared vanilla pudding before chilling.

Pumpkin Doughnuts

Here is a treat that is fun to make with people around to help... and to help eat as they come out of the deep fryer. No, they are not low in calories. Yes, they are delicious.

Yield: About 36 doughnuts.

2 eggs, beaten
1 cup sugar
1/2 cup buttermilk
1 cup canned pumpkin
2 tbsp vegetable oil
1/2 tsp ground cinnamon
1/2 tsp ground allspice
1/4-1/2 tsp ground ginger (to taste)
1 tsp ground nutmeg
2 tsp salt
1/2 tsp baking soda
4 cups cake flour
Oil for frying
Powdered sugar

Beat eggs and sugar until light and lemon-colored. Combine pumpkin, buttermilk and oil. Beat this mixture into the eggs. Combine cinnamon, allspice, ginger, nutmeg, salt, baking soda and flour and blend into liquid mixture. Cover with plastic wrap and chill in refrigerator for at least 1 hour.

Turn out onto a floured cutting board and roll or pat to about 1/2 inch thickness. Cut with doughnut cutter that has been dipped in flour before each cut.

Heat oil in deep fat fryer or deep kettle to 375 degrees Fahrenheit (use a thermometer to make sure you have the right temperature... if oil is not hot enough, doughnuts will be soggy; if it is too hot, they will not cook before burning on the outside). Drop doughnuts a few at a time into the hot oil, don't overload the fryer or the temperature of the oil will be reduced.

Turn each doughnut as soon as it rises to the top of the oil and remove from oil when golden brown on both sides. Drain on paper towels and dust with powdered (or granulated) sugar.

Pumpernickel Bread

Here a good firm loaf that lends itself well to sandwiches and hors d'oeuvres. Serve it warm with a bowl of homemade vegetable soup for a winter weekend supper.

Yield: 2 loaves
Oven setting: 375 degrees Fahrenheit

- 2 pkgs dry yeast
- 1 tbsp sugar
- 1 tbsp salt
- 1 tbsp oil
- 1 1/2 cups **warm water** (about 100 degrees Fahrenheit)
- 2 cups **rye flour**
- 2 cups **whole wheat flour**
- 2 1/2 cups **white bread flour**

In a large bowl, combine yeast, sugar, salt, oil and water and mix together to dissolve the sugar and salt. Combine the rye, whole wheat and white flours and then add to the water mixture. Using your hands, mix together until well blended. (If necessary, add more flour until mixture is not longer sticky.)

Turn out onto a board lightly dusted with flour and knead until smooth, about 10 minutes. Oil a large bowl and place the dough in it, turning to bring up the oiled side. Cover with a dry towel and put in a warm place to rise for 1 hour.

Punch the dough down, place it on a lightly floured board and cover with a dry towel. Allow the dough to rest for 10 minutes. Cut the dough into two parts and shape into loaves. (If you are going to bake in loaf pans, use 9x5-inch pans and grease the pans before putting the loaves in.) Cover the loaves with a dry towel and return to a warm place to raise until well rounded, about 30 minutes more.

Bake at 375 for 1 hour (when you tap the loaf and it has a hollow sound, it is done).

Pantry Soup

Here is a hearty soup that you can put together from things you usually have on hand in the cupboard and freezer. Feel free to vary the ingredients as you like... add some fresh chopped celery or parsley, for instance. If you cook for someone who has a restricted sodium intake, you should be aware, however, that because of the canned soups and juice, this soup is relatively high in salt.

Yield: 6 servings

- 1 pound lean ground beef
- 1/2 medium onion
- 1 24-ounce can mixed vegetable juice
- 1 can undiluted cream of celery soup
- 1 can undiluted cream of mushroom soup
- 1 12-ounce pkg frozen mixed vegetables

Break ground beef up and saute until lightly browned. Remove from the skillet with slotted spoon and place into a large pan.

Chop onion. In the same skillet, saute the chopped onion in the beef drippings and scrape into the pan with the cooked ground beef. Add vegetable juice, and undiluted celery and mushroom soups to the pan and mix well.

Bring mixture to a boil and add frozen mixed vegetables (and anything else you would like to add).

Reduce heat and simmer for about 10 minutes (test by tasting a green bean, if it is done, everything is).

Almond-Bacon Rice Pilaf

Rice pilaf is an excellent addition to many meals. This version is particularly good with roast turkey or with beef dishes because of its robust flavor. It is good enough, in fact, to stand on its own as a main dish casserole for a light supper.

Yield: 4-6 servings depending on how it is used

8 slices of bacon (as lean as possible)
1 cup brown rice (brown rice is better in this recipe than white)
1/4 cup slivered almonds
1/2 cup chopped green onion (include the green part too)
1/2 cup finely chopped celery
1 cup coarsely chopped mushrooms
1 tbsp soy sauce

Saute the bacon slices. Remove the slices to a paper towel to drain and cool. Remove 3 tbsp of the bacon drippings and set aside. Put the rice in the same skillet and saute very lightly, stirring constantly to coat with the bacon drippings. Scrape the rice into a sauce pan and add 1 3/4 cup boiling water. Simmer until rice is tender (about 20-25 minutes).

When the bacon is cool, crumble it into small pieces.

While the rice is cooking, put the 3 tbsp of bacon drippings you removed back into the skillet and add the almonds, about half of the chopped green onion, all of the celery and mushrooms. Cook until the almonds have turned a golden brown, stirring gently but constantly.

When the rice has cooked, add it to the vegetables and nuts with the crumbled bacon pieces. Stir all together to mix and heat through. Stir in the soy sauce (taste and add a little more soy sauce if you like). Turn into a serving dish and sprinkle the rest of the chopped green onions on the top to serve.

Refrigerator Pineapple Dessert

This is a somewhat delicate dessert of the sort that ladies used to serve in the afternoon after a game of bridge, and possibly still do. It's too good to be limited to that though. It makes a nice "after" party dessert... after a movie, after a concert, for instance.

Yield: 8 to 10 servings

> 1 1-pound box of vanilla wafers
> 3/4 cup butter/margarine
> 3 cups powdered sugar
> 3 eggs
> 1 tsp vanilla extract
> 1 tsp almond extract
> 2 cups whipping cream
> 2 tbsp sugar
> 1 tbsp lemon juice
> 2 cups drained crushed pineapple

The day before you plan to serve, butter 9x12-inch baking pan.

Crush vanilla wafers in blender, food processor or with a rolling pin. Use half of the wafers to form a bottom layer in the pan. Using an electric mixer, cream butter/margarine and powdered sugar together.

Separate eggs. Add yolks, vanilla extract and almond extract to butter-sugar mixture and beat well. Beat whites till stiff and fold into the mixture. Pour this combination over the vanilla wafer crumbs in the pan.

Whip the cream, gradually adding sugar and lemon juice. Fold in drained crushed pineapple. Spread over egg mixture. Top with the remainder of the vanilla wafer crumbs. Cover loosely with plastic wrap and chill in refrigerator for 24 hours before serving.

Really Red Devil's Food Cake

Is there anyone who doesn't love a good chocolate cake? This is a very good one. The addition of the food coloring changes the color of the cake to a rich maroon. When frosted with a white frosting the contrast is very attractive. You'll notice too that it does not call for baking powder but uses baking soda and buttermilk instead. The buttermilk, by the way, also sharpens the taste slightly.

Yield: Two-layer 8-inch cake
Oven setting: 350 degrees Fahrenheit

1/2 cup shortening
1 1/2 cups sugar
2 eggs
2 ounces red food coloring
2 tbsp dry unsweetened cocoa
1 tsp salt
2 1/2 cups cake flour
1 cup buttermilk
2 tsp vanilla
1 tbsp vinegar
1 tsp baking soda

Preheat oven to 350 degrees Fahrenheit. Butter two 8-inch cake pans and dust with flour. Set aside.

Using your electric mixer, mix shortening and sugar together until they are creamy, smooth and light. Add eggs one at a time and beat well after adding each one. In a separate small bowl, make a paste of the red food coloring and cocoa. Add the cocoa paste to the egg mixture. Mix flour and salt together. Mix buttermilk and vanilla together. Add the dry ingredients to the egg mixture alternately with the buttermilk mixture. Beat for 2 minutes after all ingredients have been added. Mix in the vinegar and baking soda.

Pour into the prepared cake pans and bake at 350 degrees for about 35 minutes or until the cakes pull away from the sides of the pans slightly. Turn the cakes out onto cooling racks and cool completely.

Split each layer in half: Take a length of dental floss and loop it around the layer. Cross the two ends and pull. As you tighten the floss it will gently cut through the layer and you will have two even halves.

Frost with butter cream frosting.

Dirty Rice

Not a very appetizing name for a dish, but one that has stuck to this rice/meat combination developed by Cajun cooks. The Tabasco sauce is a great variable in this recipe... use a little if you just want to brighten the flavor a bit, add as much more as your palate calls for (that can be an astonishing amount for some people). Extra Tabasco can also be added by the person eating the dish so if you cook for people with varying tastes in "heat", use a smaller amount and let each adjust by adding more if they choose.

Yield: 4 servings

**1/2 pound butter/margarine
1 pound lean ground beef
1 pound chicken livers, chopped
1 cup chopped onion
1/2 cup chopped green pepper
1/2 cup chopped celery
2 cloves finely chopped garlic
1/2 tsp salt
1/4 tsp *Tabasco* sauce** (more if you like)
**1/4 tsp dried thyme
1/4 tsp dried basil
2 cups cooked long grain white rice
2 tbsp chopped parsley
1/4 cup chopped green onions including green**

Melt half of the butter/margarine in a skillet and add ground beef and chopped chicken livers. Cook until browned. Transfer to a casserole. In the same pan melt the remaining butter/margarine and add the chopped onions, green peppers, celery, garlic, and seasonings. Saute until vegetables are tender and add to meat in casserole. Mix in cooked rice, parsley and green onions. If necessary, warm briefly in oven or microwave. If it seems too dry, add a little chicken broth or water.

Fruited Rice Curry Mix

This is particularly good with chicken or ham. It is one of those mixes that is handy to have in your cupboard for those dinners when you would like a little something special, but don't have time to fix something from scratch.

Yield: About 2 cups of mix

- **1 cup long grain brown rice**
- **2 tsp curry powder**
- **1 tsp powdered cumin**
- **1 tsp onion powder**
- **1/2 tsp salt**
- **1/4 cup raisins** (either dark or golden)
- **2 tbsp dried minced onion**
- **2 tsp beef bouillon granules**
- **1/4 chopped dried apricots** (or a mixture of dried apricots and apples)

Mix all ingredients together and store in an air-tight container. Use within a month or so.

To prepare:

Yield: About 4 cups of cooked curried rice.

- **2 cup of the rice mix**
- **3 1/2 cups water**
- **2 tbsp butter/margarine**
- **1/2 cup chopped peanuts**

Combine the curry rice mixture with the water and butter/margarine. Cover tightly. Bring to boil and reduce heat. Simmer for 25 minutes (test for doneness at this point and cook more if rice is not tender).

Sprinkle with chopped peanuts to serve.

Creamy Rice Pudding

While this is not really an "uncommon" recipe, it is one that people seem to look for. Most recipes for rice pudding tend to be somewhat dry, this is not. Using short grain rice produces a softer, stickier pudding, and cooking the rice first means that it doesn't absorb as much of the flavored custard. The result is a soft, moist and flavorful pudding.

Yield: 6 servings
Oven setting: 325 degrees Fahrenheit

   3 lightly beaten eggs
   2 cups milk
   1 1/2 cups cooked short grain white rice
   1/2 cup sugar
   1/2 cup raisins
   1 tsp vanilla
   1/2 tsp salt
   Ground cinnamon

Combine all ingredients except cinnamon in a bowl and mix together well. Pour into a 10x6-inch baking dish and sprinkle cinnamon to your taste on the top. Bake at 325 for about 30 minutes (or until a knife inserted near the center comes out clean). Can be served warm or chilled (a whipping cream topping is nice).

Quick Raised Dinner Rolls

These yeast-leavened dinner rolls can be made from scratch in just a little over an hour. In general, a higher proportion of yeast to flour allows the bread-product to raise faster but you sacrifice texture and keeping characteristics to achieve the speeded up raising time. On the other hand, by making just one pan of rolls, they will probably easily be eaten with one meal.

Yield: 9-12 rolls depending on size... an 8-inch square pan full
Oven setting: 400 degrees Fahrenheit

1 pkg dry yeast
2 tbsp sugar
1/2 tsp salt
1/2 cup warm milk
1 egg
1 tbsp melted butter/margarine
1 3/4 to 2 cups bread flour

Using mixer or food processor, blend all of the ingredients together. Place in a warm spot to raise (85-90 degree Fahrenheit location is ideal) until double (about 30 minutes). Butter an 8-inch square pan. When dough has doubled, punch down. Form into balls and place in pan. Let raise in pan for another 10-15 minutes. Bake until brown (about 15-20 minutes.)

Slow-rise Dinner Rolls

These are very dependable rolls. The dough can be made well in advance and kept in the refrigerator. The baked rolls freeze well too. By making each quarter of the recipe into a different style of roll, you will have a basket full of varieties to serve. They have a little more sugar than most which makes them nice as a breakfast roll too.

Yield: 24-28 rolls depending on style
Oven setting: 400 degrees Fahrenheit

2 cups warm water (90 to 100 degrees Fahrenheit)
2 pkg yeast
6 1/2-7 cups bread flour
1/2 cup sugar
2 tsp salt
1 egg
1/4 cup shortening

Mix warm water and yeast together. Add half flour, sugar and salt and beat until well mixed (a heavy-duty mixer or food processor is useful here). Add egg and shortening and gradually add the rest of the flour. Knead for about five minutes. Put into oiled bowl. Cover with damp cloth and refrigerate. Divide into quarters next day (or up to three or four days later).

Shape the rolls as suggested below. Brush with milk and top with seeds as desired. Allow to raise at room temperature 1 to 2 hours. Grease baking pans as necessary and bake for 12-15 minutes at 400 degrees Fahrenheit.

Rolls may be shaped a variety of ways:

Form small balls and put 3 in each muffin cup.

Roll larger ball in butter then in sesame seeds.

Shape into ropes about 1/2 inch in diameter and 8 inches long, make a loop and pull end through to make a knot.

Roll quarter of dough into a circle and spread with soft butter, cut into wedges and roll to form crescents.

Roquefort Dressing

There are many recipes for Roquefort (or Blue Cheese) salad dressing, but often it seems that the vinegar dominates the flavor to the exclusion of everything else. This version has a more mellow flavor and one that allows the tang of the ripened cheese to come through.

Yield: About 1 cup

    1 tbsp white wine vinegar
    2 tbsp orange juice
    1/2 cup olive oil
    1/4 cup mild oil (corn or sunflower)
    6 ounces Roquefort cheese
    1 tbsp sour cream
    1 tsp very finely minced shallots

You need a whisk for this recipe.

In a smallish bowl combine the vinegar and orange juice. In a measuring cup combine the two oils. Place the bowl on a wet towel (to hold it firmly) and slowly pour the oils in a very fine stream into the vinegar and juice while you whisk the mixture constantly. You will have an opaque, slightly thickened mixture when you finish. (This kind of mixture of oil and water is called an emulsion by chemists.)

Crumble the cheese into small bits. Take about two-thirds of the cheese and press it through a sieve to smooth it out. Blend the cheese and the sour cream until well blended and smooth. Add the minced shallots.

Add the oil/vinegar emulsion a little at a time and beat well after each addition so that it is thoroughly mixed. Cover and chill for 4 hours before using (well, at least 2 hours).

Rum Cake

This is a favorite at holiday time when the rum flavor seems to be especially appropriate for some reason. It is equally good during spring, summer, and fall... Because it is based on a cake mix, this is an easy dessert to prepare. The only tricky part is pouring the glaze so that it is absorbed by the cake, which takes time, patience and a steady hand.

Yield: About 10 servings
Oven setting: 325 degrees Fahrenheit

For the cake:

>   1/2 finely chopped walnuts (or pecans)
>   (at Holiday time you can also add 1/2 cup finely chopped
>   mixed candied fruit)
>   1 pkg yellow cake mix
>   1 pkg instant vanilla pudding
>   4 eggs
>   1/2 cup cold water
>   1/2 cup mild vegetable oil
>   1/2 cup rum

For the glaze:

>   1/4 cup butter/margarine
>   1/4 cup water
>   3/4 cup sugar
>   1/3 cup rum

To make the cake:

Prepare a 10-inch tube pan (or 12 cup Bundt pan) by buttering and then dusting with flour. Mix the chopped nuts and chopped candied fruit if you are using both. Scatter the mixture in the bottom of the baking pan and press them down lightly.

Combine the cake mix, pudding mix, eggs, water, oil, and rum in a large bowl and beat with an electric mixer for 3 minutes at medium speed. Pour into the pan on top of the nuts (and fruit). Bake at 325 for about 1 hour or until the cake starts to pull away from the sides of the pan. (Check at 50 minutes and then at 10 minute intervals until done.) Leave the cake in the pan for 10 minutes and then turn out onto a cooling rack and cool to room temperature.

To glaze the cake:

While the cake is cooling, make the glaze. Melt the butter in a small pan. Stir in water and sugar and simmer gently for 5 minutes while you slowly stir. Remove from heat and add the rum. Cool to lukewarm.

Put some waxed paper or foil under the cake cooling rack. With a skewer or clean wire, make holes through the cake. Very slowly pour the glaze over the cake, allow the cake to absorb as you pour, don't just let it run down the sides or most of it will end up on the waxed paper or foil instead of the cake. Use all of the glaze. Transfer to a serving plate.

Salsa

There are dozens of recipes for salsa. This particular one uses ingredients that you probably have in your pantry, you are especially likely to have them if you enjoy Mexican cooking at all. This salsa is not meant to be canned and stored, but rather to be refrigerated and eaten "fresh".

Yield: About 2 quarts (ingredients can be halved to make less)

2 28-ounce cans of tomatoes
1 lemon
4 7-ounce cans of diced green chili peppers
1 6-ounce can of tomato paste
1/2 cup chopped green pepper
2 tbsp unsweetened cocoa
1 1/2 tsp ground cumin
2 tbsp ground coriander

Coarsely chop the tomatoes. Remove the top and bottom ends from the lemon and chop the whole lemon into small pieces. Combine all of the ingredients in a large bowl. In the top of your blender, puree about 2 cups of the mixture at a time until all has been processed. Taste the sauce and if necessary add a bit of salt (although canned tomatoes are quite salty so you may not need any more).

The sauce should be stored in the refrigerator and used within a week. It may be frozen for longer storage but is not as good when thawed as it was before freezing.

Sangria

Sangria is a lovely wine punch of Spanish origin that is spicy and flavorful. It seems just right for a warm summer evening. For an added touch, it is attractive to carefully remove the zest from an orange in one long piece and place it in the pitcher used to serve the sangria.

Yield: 4 servings

> **1/2 cup water**
> **1 cup sugar**
> **1 whole cinnamon stick**
> **1 lemon**
> **1 orange**
> **1/2 cup orange juice**
> **1/4 cup lemon juice**
> **1 fifth full-bodied red wine** (such as zinfandel, barbera, or
>   a good quality "jug wine" burgundy)

Mix water, sugar, and cinnamon together in a saucepan. Bring to boil, lower heat and simmer for 10 minutes, stirring constantly to dissolve sugar. Strain and cool. Slice lemon. Remove strips of zest from orange, peel away the white pith and slice the orange (if peaches are in season, sliced fresh peaches can be substituted for orange). Stir in cooled syrup. Let fruit marinate in syrup in refrigerator overnight.

To serve:

Add orange juice, lemon juice and wine to mixture. Put ice in pitcher and serve in wine glasses garnished with bits of fruit if you like.

Pickled Sausage Slices

This is a tasty addition to a tray of hors d'oeuvres. The slices are also good in a sandwich, especially one made on pumpernickel or dilled rye bread with a slice of Swiss cheese.

Yield: About 60 sausage rounds depending on how thick you like the slices to be

2 cups water
2 cups white vinegar (white wine vinegar is best)
3 tbsp sugar
1 tsp whole peppercorns
1 tsp whole allspice
1 tsp dill seeds
1 tsp celery seeds
1 tsp mustard seeds
5-6 fully cooked German-style sausages
1 cup thinly sliced onion

Combine water, vinegar, sugar, and spices and bring to a boil. Reduce heat and simmer for 15 minutes. Remove from heat and cool slightly.

If the sausages you use have casings (hard covering), remove that and discard. Slice the sausage diagonally in the thickness you like (not more than 1/4 inch thick is best). Using a two quart glass container, alternate layers of sausage slices and sliced onion. Pour the marinade over the layers. Cover tightly and refrigerate. Allow the sausages to marinate at least three days before using. They will keep in the refrigerator for 3-4 weeks.

Custom-seasoned Sausage

By starting with simple ground pork (or grinding your own from pork butt or shoulder), you can add seasonings to create sausages much more to your taste than any you can buy commercially. Here are a two ideas for sausage seasoning.

Sweet-Hot Italian Sausage

Yield: 1 pound of sausage

> 1 tsp fennel seeds
> 2 tsp coriander seeds
> 2 tsp dried parsley
> 1 tsp salt
> 1 garlic clove, minced
> 1/2 tsp ground pepper
> 1 pound ground pork

Using a mortar and pestle or your blender, make a powder out of the fennel seeds, coriander seeds, dried parsley, salt, minced garlic, and pepper. Add the spice mixture to the ground pork and lightly mix together using your hands. Shape the meat into a loaf and use within two days.

American Breakfast Sausage

Yield: 1 pound of sausage

> 1/4 tsp dried thyme
> 1/4 tsp dried sage
> 1/2 tsp coriander seed
> 1/2 tsp dried marjoram
> 1/2 tsp pepper
> 1 pound ground pork

Using a mortar and pestle or your blender, make a powder out of the thyme, sage, coriander seeds, marjoram and pepper. Add the spice mixture to the ground pork and lightly mix together using your hands. Shape the meat into a loaf and use within two days.

You can make sausage up in larger amounts if you like. Divide into pound portions and wrap each portion in plastic wrap and then in freezer foil. Store in your freezer and use within 3 months.

Scallop Chowder

Clam chowder is a familiar standby. Scallop chowder is not as common. This particular recipe has a tomato base similar to a New York-style clam chowder rather than a cream sauce. It is milder than clam chowder and, because the scallops are themselves larger than clams, seems meatier. Anyone who likes fish chowders of any kind will certainly like this!

Yield: 4 generous servings, 6 in small bowls (with no seconds)

6 slices bacon
1 onion
2 carrots
1 green pepper
3 medium potatoes
3 1/2 cups canned tomatoes
1 cup tomato juice
1 tsp salt
1/2 tsp dry thyme (1 tsp fresh)
1 tsp Worcestershire sauce
1 pound sea scallops
Chopped fresh parsley (and fresh basil if available)

Cut bacon into small pieces and cook. Chop onion, carrot and pepper into small pieces. Remove bacon pieces from skillet and add chopped vegetables. Cook until onion is limp and golden.

Meanwhile dice potatoes and cook until tender. Add tomatoes, tomato juice, salt, and thyme to sauteed vegetables and cook for 10 minutes. Just before serving time, add potatoes to tomato mixture. Stir in Worcestershire sauce and bring to just under a boil. If scallops are large, you can cut them into smaller pieces. Add scallops and cook until scallops are just opaque. (Don't over-cook or scallops can become tough.) Garnish with chopped parsley and basil and serve immediately.

Scripture Cake

This is one of those recipes that you see requested from time to time in newspaper food sections. It is a bit of a novelty because of the context. The cake itself is a spice cake, a little on the heavy side.

Yield: 10-12 servings
Oven setting: 300 degrees Fahrenheit

1 cup Judges 5:25 (butter)
1 3/4 cup Jeremiah 6:20 (sugar)
1/4 cup Proverbs 24:13 (honey)
6 Job 39:14 (eggs)
First Kings 10:2 (spices: 2 tsp ground cinnamon, 1/2 tsp ground cloves, 1 1/2 tsp ground allspice, 1 tsp ground nutmeg)
3 tsp Amos 4:5 (leavening: baking powder, plus 1 tsp baking soda)
1 tsp Leviticus 2:13 (salt)
3 3/4 cups First Kings 4:22 (unsifted flour)
1 cup First Samuel 30:12, first phrase (chopped dried figs)
2 cups First Samuel 30:12, second phrase (raisins)
1 cup Numbers 17:8 (chopped almonds)
1 cup Genesis 24:11 (water)

Preheat oven to 300 degrees Fahrenheit. Generously grease and flour a 10-inch tube pan.

With an electric mixer, beat butter until light and then slowly add sugar and cream together until light colored. Add honey. Beat in eggs one at a time mixing well after each addition. Mix together dry ingredients. Take out a half cup of the mixture and toss with raisins, figs, and nuts. Add remainder of dry ingredients to egg-butter-sugar mixture alternately with water. By hand, fold nuts and fruit into batter. Pour into pan.

Bake for about 1 1/2 hours (or until a cake is firm to touch on top). Let cool in pan for 1/2 hour and then turn out onto cooling rack. Let cool completely before cutting.

Seafood Casserole

This might be called a baked seafood salad, but most of us think of salads has being cold and casseroles being hot. Whatever you want to call it, this is a delicious dish that works particularly well for a buffet. Amounts may be increased proportionally for more servings.

Yield: 4 servings
Oven setting: 350 degrees Fahrenheit

- 1 cup uncooked long grain white or brown rice
- 1 cup finely chopped celery
- 1/2 cup chopped green pepper
- 1 6-ounce can of sliced water chestnuts
- 1/2 pound crab meat (canned, fresh or frozen crab meat, or imitation crab meat)
- 1/2 pound cooked small shrimp
- 1 cup mayonnaise (use regular mayonnaise, not the reduced-calorie version)
- 1/2 cup tomato juice
- 1/2 cup dry bread crumbs
- 1/2 cup grated Parmesan cheese
- 2 tbsp melted butter/margarine

Combine rice with 1 3/4 cup boiling water, cover and cook until the rice is tender.

Combine cooked rice with chopped celery, chopped green pepper, sliced water chestnuts, crab, shrimp, mayonnaise, and tomato juice. Turn out into a 2-quart oven-safe casserole.

Combine crumbs, parmesan cheese and melted butter/margarine and use this mixture to cover the top of the casserole.

Bake at 350 degrees Fahrenheit for 30 minutes.

Seasoning Salt Mix

Here is an all-purpose seasoning salt than can be used with everything from salads to barbecued meats to vegetables. Using the extra herbs means that by volume there is less salt, something that many people will favor.

Yield: About 2/3 cup seasoning salt

> 6 tbsp table salt
> 1/2 tsp dried thyme
> 1/2 tsp garlic powder
> 1/2 tsp onion powder
> 1/2 tsp dried lemon rind
> 2 tsp paprika
> 2 tsp dry mustard
> 1/2 curry powder
> 1/2 tsp powdered cumin

Put all ingredients into blender container and process at a low speed until well blended. Put into shaker (this is a good way to recycle a spice container).

Use in salads and with vegetables, also good on meats and fish.

Herb Seasoning Mixes

For some people it is important for salt to be restricted. Mixtures you put together from dried herbs make a very acceptable substitute. Because you blend them yourself, you can proportion the herbs to your taste... here are some suggestions that seem to work well.

For Chicken:

Combine equal parts of tarragon, parsley, marjoram, and savory.

For Eggs:

Combine equal parts of chives, parsley, and marjoram.

For Fish:

Combine equal parts of dill, chives, lemon balm (or dried lemon zest), and tarragon.

For Beef:

Combine equal parts of thyme, basil, and savory.

For Pork:

Combine equal parts of sage, basil, and savory.

For Lamb:

Combine equal parts of rosemary, thyme, marjoram, and parsley.

For Potatoes:

Combine equal parts of rosemary, oregano, thyme, and pepper.

Seed Cake

This is a very old recipe... references to earliest versions of it show up in medieval manuscripts. It is a simple cake, spicy in flavor and delicious. We do not often think of caraway as a spice used in desserts but it gives the cake a unique flavor and fragrance. This is typically served without frosting.

Yield: about 8 servings
Oven setting: 350 degrees Fahrenheit

1/2 cup softened butter (butter is best in this)
2/3 cup sugar
2 tsp caraway seeds
2 eggs
1 1/4 cups all-purpose flour
3 tbsp cornstarch
1/2 tsp baking powder
1 tsp ground cinnamon
1/4 tsp ground cloves

Prepare a small round cake pan, 6 inches in diameter and about 3 inches high if you have one. If you don't have a cake pan of those dimensions, look through your casseroles and see if you have one about that size. You can use your standard 8 or 9-inch cake pans, the cake will taste the same but not be quite as traditional in appearance.

Mix butter and sugar together until they are light and creamy. Add the caraway seeds and mix them into the butter-sugar mixture.

Beat the eggs and add them to the mixture a little at a time, mixing well as you go.

Mix together the flour, cornstarch, baking powder, cinnamon and cloves. Fold them into the batter using a u-shaped motion and continue folding until dry ingredients are all combined, but do in gently. Carefully pour batter into your prepared baking pan or casserole.

If you are using a 6-inch pan, it will take about 1 1/4 to 1 1/2 hours to bake at 350. Using a standard 8 or 9-inch cake pan will cut the baking time to between about 45 minutes and 1 hour. The cake is done when it starts to pull away from the sides of the pan. Cool for 10 minutes in the pan and then turn out to cool on a cooling rack.

Flavored Seven Minute Frosting

Seven minute frosting has been around for a long time. Its greatest drawback is that it is fine if you frost and serve the cake immediately, but it just doesn't keep well. A second problem is that it normally has a very bland flavor. Here is a way to solve both problems... with a bonus of adding a lovely color to the frosting too.

Yield: Enough to frost a double layer cake, a 10-inch tube cake, or about 2 dozen cupcakes

2 egg whites
1 1/4 cups sugar
1 3-ounce package of flavored gelatin dessert (your choice of flavors)
1/8 tsp salt
1/3 cup water
1 tbsp white corn syrup

Combine unbeaten egg whites, sugar, flavored gelatin, salt, water, and corn syrup in the top portion of a double boiler. Using a portable electric hand mixer (or old fashioned rotary egg beater), beat the mixture until it is very well mixed (a minute or two).

Place the pan over simmering water in the bottom portion of the double boiler and continue to beat at high speed until the frosting will stand in stiff peaks (this will take about 7 minutes, hence the name). Occasionally use a spoon to stir the frosting from the bottom and sides of the pan so that it is all included in the beating.

Remove the pan from above the boiling water and continue to beat for another minute or so, or until the frosting is thick enough to spread.

Marinated Shrimp

Marinated shrimp make a very pretty addition to a buffet table as an appetizer or as a garnish for a green salad. Serve them with crackers as an hors d'oeuvres too.

Yield: 4-6 appetizer servings

- **1 pound cooked medium shrimp** (shells removed and deveined)
- **1/4 cup French vermouth**
- **2 small cloves of garlic, finely chopped**
- **4 green onions including green parts, finely chopped**
- **1 tbsp dry tarragon** (about 3 tbsp fresh tarragon)
- **1/2 tsp salt**
- **1/2 tsp whole peppercorns** (green peppercorns are nice)
- **1 tsp Dijon mustard**
- **2 tbsp white wine vinegar**
- **1/2 cup olive oil**

Put the shrimp in a jar large enough to hold both shrimp and marinade (this recipe makes something less than a cup of marinade).

Make the marinade by combining vermouth, garlic, green onions and tarragon in a small saucepan. Simmer for about 2 or 3 minutes then remove from heat and stir in the remaining ingredients and pour over the shrimp.

Allow to marinate for at least 24 hours before using and will keep for 3-4 days in your refrigerator.

Pickled Shrimp

These have quite a different flavor from the Marinated Shrimp version... the additional vinegar makes a big difference in the taste.

Yield: 10 appetizer servings, more if combined with other appetizers

2 1/2 pounds fresh medium shrimp
1 large onion
1 lemon
6 bay leaves
3/4 cup mild salad oil
3/4 cup olive oil
3/4 cup white wine vinegar
2 1/2 tsp celery seed
Pepper sauce to taste
1 tsp salt
2 1/2 tbsp capers (optional)

Remove shells, clean, and cook the shrimp. Cut the onion and lemon into thin slices and toss together. Alternate layers of shrimp with the onion-lemon slice mixture. Put a bay leaf or two on each layer of shrimp. Combine oils, vinegar, celery seed, pepper sauce, salt, and capers and pour over layered shrimp. Allow to marinate for 24 hours.

Drain well and serve chilled.

Sirniki

This is a dish with its origins in Russia. It makes a lovely brunch entree, and also can serve as a late-night supper dish because it's not too heavy. If you can't find dry curd cottage cheese, rinse regular small curd cottage. cheese in cold water and press the liquid out using a sieve or colander. Keep the curds as intact as possible though.

Yield: 4 servings

3 cups dry curd cottage cheese
2 eggs
2 tbsp sour cream
2/3 cup all-purpose flour
Salt to taste
Flour
1/4 cup butter (butter is better in this recipe than margarine)
Sour cream
Fruit: fresh strawberries or other berries, or fresh peaches or nectarines. You can also use cooked apple slices or plums, or cranberry sauce.

Mix the cottage cheese, eggs, 2 tbsp sour cream, flour and salt together. Using your hands, form the batter into balls about the size of a golf ball and put the balls on a lightly floured surface. Dust with flour and flatten to about 3/4 inch thickness. Dust with a little more flour.

Melt the butter in a large skillet and saute the cottage cheese cakes on both sides.

Serve with sour cream and the fruit you have selected.

Smoked Salmon Mousse

Smoked salmon, or lox as it is sometimes called, is wonderful tasting, but very expensive. In this appetizer, you use enough smoked salmon to add plenty of flavor but augment it with canned salmon. Use a pretty mold and it will be the talk of the party.

Yield: 4 cup mousse, about 15 appetizer servings

1 16-ounce can of salmon
1/4 pound smoked salmon (lox)
1 tbsp unflavored gelatin
1/4 cup cold water
1/3 cup boiling water
1/3 cup sour cream
1/3 cup mayonnaise
2 tbsp finely chopped onion
1 tbsp finely chopped parsley
1 tbsp dried dill
1 tbsp lemon juice
1/2 tsp salt
1/8 tsp *Tabasco* **sauce**
1 cup whipping cream

Remove skin and bones from canned salmon and flake into small pieces. Chop smoked salmon into small pieces too.

In a large bowl combine gelatin and cold water and allow gelatin to soften for 5 minutes. Slowly stir in boiling water and stir until gelatin is dissolved. Refrigerate to cool to luke warm.

Add sour cream, mayonnaise, onion, parsley, dill, lemon juice, salt, and *Tabasco* to gelatin and mix well. Return to refrigerator and chill until mixture will mound (15-30 minutes depending on temperature when it is put back into the refrigerator). While gelatin mixture is thickening, whip cream in a chilled bowl.

When gelatin mixture has thickened sufficiently to mound slightly when spooned, mix in canned and smoked salmon. Fold in whipped cream.

Lightly spread the inside of a 4-cup mold with vegetable oil and pour the mousse into it. Cover with plastic wrap and chill for at least 4, preferably 6 hours.

To serve, turn the mold out onto a serving platter and garnish with fresh dill if you have it, if not garnish with parsley sprigs.

Sourdough Starter

It is said that there are sourdough yeast cultures that are literally generations old and that is certainly possible. The old prospectors and settlers were glad to have a long-lived source for leavening their biscuits and pancakes and they cherished their sourdough yeast starters.

It really isn't hard to get a culture going though, especially if you use commercial yeast rather than relying on often unpredictable and unreliable "wild" yeast to get started.

Yield: About 2 cups of starter

2 cups flour
2 tbsp sugar
1 package dry yeast
1/2 tsp salt
2 cups warm water

Combine all of the ingredients and mix until smooth. Keep at room temperature for 3 days, stirring at least three times a day, oftener if you are able to do so. After 3 days, store in the refrigerator in a tightly covered container.

To use, stir the sourdough starter and remove the amount your recipe calls for. Replenish the starter by adding that same amount in a combination of flour and water mixed together. Each time you replenish the mixture, let the container stay at room temperature for a day before using. (There is a recipe for Sourdough Bread on the next page.)

Sourdough baked goods are wonderful... not only bread and pancakes, but also waffles, muffins, cakes and many other good things.

Sourdough Bread

Now you have your sourdough starter, try it out by making a loaf of wonderfully fragrant sourdough bread...

Yield: 4 loaves
Oven setting: 400 degrees Fahrenheit

1/2 cup sourdough starter
1 cup warm water (about 90 degrees Fahrenheit)
4 to 4 1/2 cups bread flour (all-purpose flour can be used)
1 tsp sugar
1 tsp salt
1/2 cup buttermilk
1/4 cup milk
1 tbsp butter/margarine
1 egg white beaten with 1 tbsp water
Cornmeal

Remove your sourdough starter from the refrigerator and stir it well. Take out 1/2 cup of the starter and place it in a large, bowl that you have warmed by rinsing in hot water.

Add the warm water to the sourdough starter and mix. Add 1 1/2 cups flour and beat the batter for about 5 minutes. Cover the bowl with plastic wrap and leave it in a warm place for 12 hours.

Stir the batter well and remove 1/2 cup of the starter to replenish the starter base. Stir this 1/2 cup of new starter into the old and return the replenished starter to the refrigerator.

Mix the sugar, salt, and 1/2 cup flour together and add to the batter. Mix in well.

Combine the buttermilk and milk in a small pan and warm to lukewarm. Add the butter/margarine and stir until melted. Add the milk combination to the batter and stir in well. Stir in 2 more cups of flour.

Turn out onto a lightly floured board and knead the dough until it is smooth and elastic. This will take about 10 minutes and you will add about 1/2 to 1 cup more flour while you do this kneading. Shape the kneaded dough into a ball and place the ball in a large bowl that has been well oiled in advance. Turn the ball so that an oiled side is up. Cover with plastic wrap and put it in a warm place to raise for about 2 hours or until it has doubled in size.

Punch the dough down, turn it again, re-cover it with the plastic wrap and allow it to raise for one more hour.

Turn the dough out onto a floured board and punch it down. Cover with a dry towel and allow it to rest for 10 minutes.

Divide the dough into 4 parts and shape each part into a long loaf. Sprinkle two cookie sheets with cornmeal and place the shaped loaves on the cookie sheets. Do not place them too close together. Cover the loaves with a dry towel and allow them to raise until doubled one more time. This should take less than an hour.

With a sharp knife, make 3 or 4 diagonal slashes in the top of each loaf, cutting down about 1/2 inch into the dough. Brush the loaves with the egg white-water mixture (use your hands to smooth the water all over the dough). Bake at 400 for about 30 minutes or until the crust is golden brown. Place on racks to cool.

Spaghetti Pie

There is something about many pasta-based main dishes that put them in the category we call "comfort foods". This recipe is one of those. It is a dish that kids seem to like a lot.

Yield: 6 generous servings
Oven setting: 350 degrees Fahrenheit

> 1 pound lean ground beef, or 1/2 pound each lean ground
>   beef and Italian sausage
> 1/2 cup chopped onion
> 1/4 cup chopped green pepper
> 1 cup chopped tomatoes (canned or peeled fresh)
> 1 6-ounce can of tomato paste
> 1 tsp sugar
> 1 tsp dried oregano
> 1 tsp dried basil
> 1 clove garlic minced
> 2 eggs
> 6 ounces dry spaghetti*
> 2 tbsp butter/margarine
> 1/3 cup grated Parmesan cheese
> 1 cup ricotta cheese (or small curd cottage cheese)
> 1/2 cup shredded mozzarella cheese

*Make a circle of your thumb and forefinger about 1 1/2 inches in diameter, the amount of dry spaghetti that you can hold in that space will be about 6 ounces.

Crumble and cook the ground beef (or ground beef/sausage mixture) until lightly browned then add onion and green pepper. Drain off excess oil. Add chopped tomatoes and liquid, tomato paste, sugar, oregano, basil, and garlic to mixture. Cook until heated throughout and keep warm. Butter a 10-inch pie pan (one that has at least a two inch depth). Beat the eggs until well mixed. Cook spaghetti al dente and drain. While the spaghetti is hot, mix it with the butter/margarine, Parmesan cheese and eggs. Spread the mixture across the bottom and push it up the sides of the pie pan to form a "crust". Spread the ricotta or cottage cheese over the bottom of the pie "shell" and add the meat mixture. Bake at 350 for 20 minutes. Remove from oven and top with shredded mozzarella cheese. Bake 5 minutes more (or until cheese melts). Let stand for 5 to 10 minutes before cutting into wedges to serve.

Spice or Herb Jelly

Excellent jellies can be made using either spices in your cupboard or herbs you have grown for flavoring. Some specific combinations that work well include: grape juice with fresh tarragon, apple juice with mint or stick cinnamon, orange juice with marjoram or whole allspice, cranberry juice with rosemary or whole cloves. Experiment yourself ... you may find some other interesting combinations.

Yield: About 4 half-pint jars

- **3 cups juice**
- **1/4 cup fresh herb, or 2 tbsp whole spices** (3 sticks cinnamon)
- **2 tbsp wine or cider vinegar**
- **3 cups sugar**
- **3 ounces liquid pectin** (1 pouch or half of 1 bottle)
- **Food coloring** (optional)
- **Paraffin**

Bring 1 cup of juice to a full boil and pour over herb or spice and let it steep for 30 minutes. Strain into a large pan. Add remaining 2 cups of juice, vinegar and sugar. Mix well and bring to a full boil stirring constantly. Stir in pectin and boil for 1 minute continuing to stir constantly. Remove from heat and stir in food coloring if you are using it.

Immediately pour into sterilized glasses and cover with a thin layer of paraffin. Store in a cool dry place.

Spinach Cheesecake Appetizer

This is the sort of appetizer that is served separately as a first course at the table. It also works well for a buffet service but is a little too rich to use as you might use a spinach souffle. Sometimes it is nice to serve just a variety of appetizers to guests for a light supper. This recipe would work particularly well in that setting.

Yield: 12 appetizer servings
Oven setting: 350 degrees Fahrenheit

> **24 ounces** (1 1/2 pounds) **cream cheese**
> **1 10-ounce pkg frozen spinach**
> **1/4 cup melted butter/margarine**
> **1 1/2 cup fine dry bread crumbs**
> **1/4 cup cream**
> **1/2 tsp salt**
> **1/3 tsp nutmeg**
> **1/8 tsp** *Tabasco* **sauce**
> **4 eggs**
> **4 ounces** (about 1 cup) **grated Swiss cheese**
> **1/4 cup finely chopped green onion or chives**
> **1 cup finely chopped ham**
> **3 tbsp butter/margarine**
> **1/2 pound fresh mushrooms chopped**

Remove the cream cheese from the refrigerator and allow it to soften. Preheat oven to 350 degrees Fahrenheit. Thaw spinach and drain well. Press until almost all moisture has been removed and set aside.

Combine melted butter/margarine and bread crumbs and press into the bottom and up the sides of a well-buttered 9-inch spring-form pan. Bake at 350 degrees Fahrenheit for 7-10 minutes or until lightly browned. Remove from oven and cool. Reduce oven heat to 325 degrees Fahrenheit.

Combine cream cheese, cream, salt, nutmeg and *Tabasco* sauce until well blended using a mixer, or food processor. Add eggs one at a time and mix well. Divide this mixture into two parts.

Combine one half of mixture with grated Swiss cheese and set aside. Combine other half of mixture with spinach, chopped green onions (or chives), and ham and set aside.

Melt remaining butter/margarine in saucepan, add chopped fresh mushrooms and saute until mushrooms are golden and tender. Set aside.

When crust has cooled pour spinach mixture onto crust. Next spread a layer of sauteed mushrooms on top of the spinach. Finally spread Swiss cheese mixture overall. Place cake on a baking sheet. Reduce heat to 325 degrees and bake for 1 to 1 1/2 hours, until center is firm but not hard. Turn off heat in oven but leave the cheesecake in the oven to slowly cool for another hour. Remove from oven and cool on cake rack to room temperature then chill in refrigerator.

Stuffed Squash Blossoms

There are some flowers that are edible, and delicious. Certainly among these garden bonuses are the blossoms that appear on your zucchini, pumpkin and other squash plants. Since these summer garden favorites seem always to produce a lot more squashes than we can use, this is a good way to control production and at the same time serve something a little different at your next summer buffet or cocktail party. The best blossoms to use for cooking are the large ones that grow directly from the stem of the plant.

Yield: 24 appetizer servings or 6-8 dinner servings

24 squash blossoms*
3 ounces cream cheese
1 egg yolk
1 tbsp sour cream or yogurt
1/3 cup grated hard cheese (cheddar, Swiss, provolone, or
    feta for instance)
3 tbsp fresh grated Parmesan cheese
2 tbsp chopped green onion or fresh chives
Flour
2 eggs
Salt to taste
Oil for frying

*Flowers are edible only if you have **not** used insecticides in your planting area.

Select and pick the blossoms in the early morning before it is too warm. Take a bowl of water with you. When you cut them off leave a bit of stem and immediately put the stems in the water. When you come in, cover the bowl loosely with plastic wrap and store in the refrigerator until you are ready to prepare in the evening.

To prepare, remove the internal portions of the flower and leave only the petals. Wash the flowers well to remove any dirt and bugs that may have clung to them, and cut off the stems. While you are preparing the flowers, take cream cheese from the refrigerator to soften. Mix the softened cream cheese with the single egg yolk, sour cream (or yogurt), grated hard cheese and Parmesan. Add the green onion (or chives) and salt to taste.

Gently open each blossom and spoon in about a teaspoonful of filling. Twist the end to close.

Put some flour into a shallow dish. Beat the two eggs. Roll each filled blossom in the flour and then dip in the beaten eggs.

Heat about 1/4 inch oil in a large skillet and fry each blossom until golden brown. Drain on paper towels. Serve warm.

Brandied Strawberries

Brandied strawberries can be used in a variety of ways... over ice cream of course, but also over custards and other bland puddings, with cream cheese and crackers, or as a sauce for crepes. Jars of brandied strawberries also make a nice gift.

Yield: About 3 cups of fruit and syrup

1 dry quart measure of strawberries (buy some extras so
    that you have plenty to choose from)
1 cup brandy
2 cups sugar

Small berries work best in this recipe. Choose berries that are nicely shaped and red all over but not over-ripe. Wash, remove stems and measure to make sure you have a full quart of usable berries.

Put the berries in a jar or crock with a tight cover. Mix the brandy and sugar together and warm over low heat, stir until sugar is dissolved and then stir into berries. (Stir carefully so that berries are not cut or bruised.) Cover tightly and put them on a cupboard shelf where you see them often enough to remind yourself to stir them from time to time (about 2 or 3 times a week).

Let the berries marinate in the brandy sauce through the summer. They will give up some of their liquid and become smaller and paler in color while they are marinating. They are ready to eat in about 3 months and keep for about a year (after that time they begin to lose their flavor although they are still safe to eat).

Brandied Fresh Pineapple

Fresh pineapple can also be made into a brandied dessert sauce this way. Use 1 cup sugar for each 2 cups of chunks of fresh (peeled and eyes removed) pineapple. Mix a 1/2 cup of brandy with each cup of sugar and proceed as indicated for strawberries. Brandied pineapple is particularly good with citrus sherbet or over poached winter pears.

Strawberry Soup

This unusual cold soup is a lovely way to start a summer luncheon on the patio ...it's a bit like a liquid fruit salad!

Yield: 6 servings

2 pints fresh strawberries, cleaned and halved
1 cup orange juice
1 tbsp cornstarch
1 cup blush or rosé wine
1/2 cup sugar
Sour cream and small whole strawberries

Set aside 6 small strawberries to use as garnish. Puree the rest of the berries in blender or food processor and set aside.

Combine 1/4 cup orange juice and cornstarch in a saucepan. Add the rest of the orange juice, wine and sugar and bring to a boil. Remove from heat immediately. Combine with pureed strawberries and chill.

Serve in small bowls and top each serving with a dollop of sour cream and a small berry.

Sunshine Strawberry Preserves

These preserves are wonderful... when you pour some into a bowl on a January morning, the aroma will transport you back to June. The preserves turn out best when you use smaller berries. Consult the weather forecast before you start because it takes several sunny days to process them, but there is little for you to do after the first day.

Yield: It depends on how many you process.
Oven setting: 200 degrees Fahrenheit

> **As many fresh strawberries as you can line up on trays and cookie sheets.**
> **Sugar** (roughly by volume as much sugar as berries on a cup-for-cup basis)

Wash and remove the stems and leaves from the berries. Measure the berries out so you know how many cups you have. Place the berries in a large pan or kettle.

Measure as many cups of granulated sugar as you have cups of berries into a shallow pan and warm it in the oven. Pour the warmed sugar over the berries and gently mix them together using your hands so that the berries are not bruised.

Put the berries and sugar over a very low heat. Stir very gently from time to time until the sugar has dissolved. Then increase the heat and bring the mixture to a boil. Cook it for 5 minutes exactly then remove from the heat. Skim off the foam that will have formed on the top and cool the mixture slightly. (You may want to stir once more after 5 minutes and skim the top again.)

Using a slotted spoon, remove the berries and line them up on trays and cookie sheets in a single layer. Cook the juice for 15 minutes more and then gently pour it over the berries.

Cover the berries with sheets of plastic wrap. Leave the wrap unattached in places so that evaporation may occur. Put the platters out in full sun. (If insects are a problem for you, put strips of cheesecloth around the edges of the trays, but don't put it over the top because that will make a shadow and keep the fruit from processing.)

Take the trays in at night (and also if you should have a summer shower). It will take about 2 or 3 days for the syrup to evaporate. When it has reached the thickness you like, ladle the berries and syrup into jars and seal with paraffin.

These should be used within 6 months.

Flower Flavored Sugars

This is a very old fashioned idea, but one that is nice to revive. Flower flavored sugars can be used in ice tea, sprinkled over fruit, dusted over icing on a cake or cookies, or in punches. The flavor is gentle but delightful. A jar of flower flavored sugar makes a pleasant gift and can be dressed up by using a pretty label and putting one leaf or blossom against the glass of the jar as you pour the sugar in.

Yield: 1 cup flavored sugar

1/4 cup of fresh suitable flowers or leaves
   (rose petals, scented geranium leaves, lemon balm, various mints, lemon verbena, violets) Do not use flowers from planting areas where insecticide has been used.

1 cup super-fine sugar*

Use only one type of flower or leaf in each batch of flavored sugar. Wash and dry the flowers or leaves carefully. In an air-tight storage container, put in 1/4 inch of sugar then a layer of flowers or leaves and alternate until the sugar is used.

Cover tightly and store for three weeks. Strain out the dry leaves and pack the flavored sugar into a storage jar.

*If you cannot fine super-fine sugar to purchase, simply put granulated sugar in your blender and run for a few seconds.

Roasted and Salted Sunflower Seeds

Sunflowers are fun to grow. They also provide a small harvest of sunflower seeds to feed the wild birds and to roast for family enjoyment.

Oven setting: 350 degrees Fahrenheit

Gather the seeds in the early fall when they are dried out in the blossom and dark brown or black. Preheat oven to 350 degrees Fahrenheit. Spread seeds on a cookie sheet and bake for 10 minutes. Cool and remove shells. Return shelled seeds to the baking sheet, sprinkle lightly with salt and bake for another 10 minutes. Cool on the pan and store in a tightly covered container.

Swedish Pancakes

These are not the pancakes you get when you use a baking mix or order pancakes in a restaurant. Neither are they the delicate crepes so prized by the French. Rather they are somewhere between the two... substantial but at the same time light. They are traditionally served with lingonberries or lingonberry syrup, but are good with any fruit syrup.

Yield: 4 servings

4 eggs
2 1/2 cups milk
1/2 cup cream or half-and-half (light cream)
1 tbsp sugar
1/4 tsp salt
1 cup all-purpose flour

Combine all ingredients and beat well. Let stand for 30-60 minutes before cooking. To cook, pour about a quarter cup at a time in a crepe pan or flat skillet. Cook over moderate heat until cake is lightly browned then roll up. Keep warm while the rest are cooked.

Sweet Potato Biscuits

Would you be surprised to hear this is a southern specialty? Probably not, because a lot of good dishes using sweet potatoes come from that part of the country. In addition to being a delicious change from ordinary biscuits, the sweet potatoes make these an excellent source of vitamin A so they are good for you too!

Yield: About 36 biscuits
Oven setting: 450 degrees Fahrenheit

> **2 cups hot cooked sweet potatoes**
> **1/2 cup butter/margarine**
> **1/2 cup sugar**
> **6 tbsp buttermilk** (1/4 cup plus 2 tbsp)
> **3-4 cups all purpose flour**
> **4 tsp baking powder**
> **1/2 tsp baking soda**
> **1 tsp salt**

Preheat oven to 450 degrees Fahrenheit.

Mash sweet potatoes and combine with butter/margarine stirring until butter/margarine melts. Add sugar and buttermilk and mix well. Combine flour, baking powder, baking soda, and salt. Add to sweet potato mixture and stir until just blended (don't over mix). Scrape batter onto cutting board and roll or pat to about 1/2 inch thickness and cut into 2-inch circles with biscuit cutter or the edge of a drinking glass. Place on ungreased baking sheet (not touching if you want a crust all around, with sides together if you want soft sides). Bake for 8-10 minutes or until lightly browned.

Sweet Potato Casserole

This is always a popular dish, particularly good with ham or turkey. It is, admittedly, sweet and consequently not low in calories, but your family and guests will like it. A good choice to include in a buffet dinner.

Yield: 8 generous servings
Oven setting: 350 degrees Fahrenheit

For the casserole

> **3 eggs**
> **3 cups mashed sweet potatoes or yams**
> **1/2 cup sugar**
> **1/3 cup milk**
> **1 tbsp vanilla extract**
> **1/2 cup melted butter/margarine**

For the topping:

> **1 cup brown sugar**
> **2/3 cup flour**
> **1 cup chopped pecans**
> **1/2 cup butter/margarine**

Lightly beat the eggs. Mix the sweet potatoes or yams, sugar, milk, vanilla extract, beaten eggs, and melted butter/margarine together. Spoon into a buttered 13x9-inch baking pan or other large casserole.

Combine the brown sugar, flour, pecans and butter by blending with a pastry blender or your fingers. Sprinkle over the sweet potato mixture.

Bake at 350 degrees Fahrenheit for 30 minutes (longer if you use a casserole that is more than 2 inches deep).

Simply the Best Syrup

After you have made and tried this, you and your family will never be completely satisfied with "store-bought" syrup again. It is a flexible recipe so feel free to vary the flavorings to your taste.

Yield: About 2 1/2 cups syrup

3 cups brown sugar (one 1-pound box)
1 1/2 cups boiling water
1 or 2 cinnamon sticks, broken into pieces
1 tsp whole allspice
1/2 tsp whole cloves
Zest of one orange or one lemon
1 tsp maple extract (optional)
1/4 tsp almond extract

Mix brown sugar and water together. Add whole spices and citrus zest. Cover and let steep for several hours. Taste to see if spicy enough and if so strain into container with cover. Stir in maple and almond extracts. Store in refrigerator.
Makes about 2 cups.

Tart Shells

Individual tarts are a pretty dessert. You can use anything from apple pie filling to ice cream to fill them. Here is a way you can make these small tart shells without any special pans.

Yield: about 12 servings
Oven setting: 400 degrees Fahrenheit

2 cups all-purpose flour
1/4 cup sugar
1/2 tsp salt
2/3 cups vegetable shortening
Iced water

In a medium sized bowl, combine the flour, sugar and salt. Add the shortening and blend in using a pastry blender. When the mixture is about the texture of coarse corn meal, add the water. Use about 1/4 cup of iced water initially and mix together using your hands. Add more water a little at a time until you can make a ball of pastry that will stick together. Mix the dough lightly and don't handle it any more than you have to.

Make a pattern to cut the tarts, a circle about 4 1/2 to 5 inches in diameter. Roll the dough out to about 1/4 inch thick and, using the pattern, cut out rounds. Turn a regular sized muffin tin upside down and place the circles of dough over each section. Pinch four corners of each circle to make a cup shape. Bake at 400 degrees for 5-6 minutes, or until golden brown.

Cool to room temperature and fill as you choose.

Easy Summer Tomato Casserole

Often times you would like to have something colorful to "fill up a corner" of a dinner plate. Something not too heavy, but flavorful. This may be what you have been looking for. Easy to prepare and delicious, it goes particularly well with steaks or pork chops, but is also good with other meats and fish as well.

Yield: 6 servings
Oven setting: 350 degrees Fahrenheit

- 1/4 cup olive oil
- 2 medium onions finely chopped
- 6 large (8 small) cloves of garlic finely chopped
- 3 pounds ripe tomatoes
- 1/2 cup fresh herbs (parsley, basil, tarragon, chives, individually or in combination)
- 1/2 cup fresh soft bread crumbs
- 1/4 cup grated parmesan cheese

Heat 2 tbsp of the olive oil and cook the onions and garlic until softened but not colored. Spread onions and garlic around in the bottom of a baking dish to make about a half inch layer. Peel and slice the tomatoes into about 1/2 inch slices. Arrange the tomato slices on top of the onions and garlic in a pretty arrangement. Combine the herbs, crumbs, and parmesan cheese, and spread them on top of the tomatoes. Drizzle the remaining 2 tbsp of olive oil over it all and place (uncovered) in the oven and bake for 25 minutes.

Tomato Paste

Making tomato paste is a long process but if you have a lot more tomatoes than you anticipated having, it is an ideal way to make good use of them. It is a fine asset to have on hand for the spaghetti sauces that taste so good during the winter. You may use any variety of tomato that is suitable for canning, but the meatier varieties will cook down faster simply because there is less juice to evaporate during cooking.

Yield: About 2 quarts

15 pounds very ripe tomatoes*
4 large green peppers
4 large carrots
4 medium sized onions
3-4 cloves garlic (or more)
1 tbsp salt
1/2 cup sugar

*Check with your County Extension Agent for local varieties that are suitable for this purpose.

Wash, core, and chop tomatoes (you do not need to remove the skins). Core, remove seeds and coarsely chop the peppers. Chop carrots and onions. Mix all of the vegetables together. Using your blender or food processor, puree the vegetable ingredients a cup at a time, adding an occasional clove of garlic. When all of the vegetables have been pureed, pour the puree through a strainer and press the pulp quite dry. Discard the pulp.

In a large kettle (at least 12 quart capacity), bring the vegetable puree to a boil over medium heat stirring constantly. Reduce heat to lowest setting and continue to simmer until thick enough to mound up slightly when dropped from spoon onto a plate. This will take about 5 hours. During this time you should stir often, increasing the frequency of stirring as the mixture becomes more thick. Do not let it burn on the bottom of the kettle or the sauce will develop a burned taste throughout.

Put the tomato paste into containers and freeze. Use within 1 year.

Tomato Sauce

Here is a way to preserve the bounty of your summer tomato crop for use all year. This sauce is recommended for freezing and is not suitable for home canning unless you are using a pressure canner. It is so good, however, that the amount yielded by this recipe will not last long in in the freezers of most households where Italian food is enjoyed.

Yield: About 1 1/2 quarts sauce

4 pounds ripe tomatoes
2 medium-to-large onions, chopped
2 medium-to-large green peppers, chopped
2-5 cloves of garlic (to your taste), **chopped**
2 tbsp olive oil
1/2 tsp salt
1/2 tsp sugar
1 tsp dried basil (1 tsp fresh)
1/2 tsp dried oregano (1 tsp fresh)
1 tsp dried parsley (1 tbsp fresh)

Peel tomatoes. (Heat a large kettle of water to just boiling temperature. Drop 3 or 4 tomatoes at a time into the water. After about 3-4 minutes remove tomatoes to a colander and rinse with cold tap water. With a sharp knife, pierce the skin and peel it off.) Continue until all tomatoes are skinned. Remove core and chop tomatoes into coarse pieces.

Cook vegetables in oil until translucent and soft. Add chopped tomatoes and seasonings and stir well. Simmer for about an hour. Taste and adjust seasonings if necessary (some additional salt is sometimes needed depending on the flavor of the tomatoes). Store in a covered container in your refrigerator for up to 10 days or freeze and keep up to 8 or 9 months.

Tomato Soup (with fresh tomatoes)

Canned tomato soup has an irrevocable place in our meals... it's hard to imagine childhood without it. On the other hand, freshly made tomato soup is in a class by itself. To taste it is to taste the essence of late summer.

Yield: 6-8 servings

    3 pounds ripe tomatoes
    1 tbsp olive oil
    1/2 cup finely chopped onion
    2 cloves of garlic, finely chopped
    1 tbsp tomato paste (freeze the rest for later use)
    4 cups chicken broth
    1 tsp dry basil
    Chopped parsley or chives

Peel, quarter and remove seeds from tomatoes. Heat oil and gently cook the onion and garlic until they are softened but not colored. Add the tomatoes and tomato paste and mix well. While onions and garlic are cooking, warm the chicken stock. Add stock and basil to vegetables, cover and simmer gently for about 20 minutes (cooking longer will cause the color to fade). Put soup in blender or food processor and puree. Warm if necessary. Serve garnished with parsley or chives. This can also be served chilled with a spoonful of sour cream (or yogurt if you are concerned about calories) in the center of each serving.

Simmered Turkey

Let's start by saying that turkey is an excellent meat. It is a good protein source, not loaded with fat or cholesterol, and it is quite inexpensive. Most people like it, and there are a lot of delicious things you can do with turkey meat.

Here's more good news... it doesn't have to be roasted, watched, basted and, in general, turn into a big preparation job.

By simmering instead of roasting you gain several advantages: the meat is uniformly moist and tender; you can prepare meat for many meals at one time by dividing it to containers for your freezer; and you end up with a stockpot full of lovely turkey stock for gravies, soups, and so forth.

Here's how you do it.

12-14 pound turkey
12 cups water
2 large carrots
3 stalks of celery
1 onion, quartered
1/2 cup coarsely chopped parsley
4 tsp salt
1 tsp dried thyme (1/2 tsp if you use powdered)
1/2 tsp whole black peppercorns
1/2 tsp whole cloves

You need a very large kettle with a rack in the bottom (so the turkey won't stick to the pan). For a 12-14 pound turkey you need a kettle that will hold at least 12 quarts of water. A canning kettle will work if you don't have anything else although the metal it is made of does not heat particularly evenly.

You can also ask your butcher to cut the bird in half lengthwise through the breast bone which will allow you to cook it in two smaller kettles by dividing the other ingredients.

Remove the giblets from the whole bird and rinse the turkey well. Put the turkey and the giblets (except the liver which will overcook) into the kettle and add the water. Add the carrots, celery, onions, parsley, salt, thyme, peppercorns and cloves.

Cover and bring to a boil. Reduce the heat and simmer about 15 minutes per pound of turkey.

Cool the turkey in the broth for thirty minutes then cover and place in the refrigerator overnight.

The next day, take the turkey from the broth and remove the skin. Take the meat away from the bones, starting with the large pieces of breast meat. Cut the meat into pieces, wrap well and either refrigerate or freeze. The whole breasts slice beautifully and the other meat can be used in casseroles, sandwiches, soups, curries, creamed dishes and so forth.

Return all of the bones and the skin to the stockpot with the broth. Simmer the broth for 4-6 hours. Chill to allow the fat to rise to the top. Remove the excess fat and store in the refrigerator or freezer.

Herb-flavored Vinegars

Herb-flavored vinegars are a valuable asset to your pantry supplies. Depending on the way they are flavored, they can be used to make variety of salad dressings, to drizzle over hot vegetables and in many other useful ways.

Fresh herbs will always make a better flavored vinegar and are much preferred if you have access to them. However, during the winter, if you have no handy pots of herbs to harvest, use the dried versions.

A bottle of home-made herb-flavored vinegar also makes a welcome gift.

Yield: 1 quart of flavored vinegar

Use **red wine vinegar** with heavier flavored herbs such as oregano, thyme, savory, sage, nasturtium flowers, basil, and garlic.

Use **white wine vinegar** with lighter flavored herbs such as tarragon, lemon balm, mint, dill, chives, carnation petals.

Start with one quart of either white or red wine vinegar. Add about 1 cup of fresh herbs or 1/4 cup dried herbs. (Use a single herb or a combination of two, but not more than two because the flavor becomes confused.)

When using fresh herbs, pick the herbs early in the day and pick only from plants that have not flowered (except when using blossoms, of course). Crush the herbs and place in a glass container.

Heat vinegar until not quite boiling and pour over crushed herbs. Steep for about 3 weeks.

Strain into pretty bottles and just before capping add a sprig of appropriate herb to the bottle. Store at room temperature.

Wassail Bowl

This year-end holiday treat brings history to your table. It has been popular literally for centuries in northern Europe, especially in Scandinavia but also in the British Isles. It is a substantial drink, one that seems just right for a snowy evening. Although it is traditionally it is a holiday drink, it shouldn't be left just for Christmas time... it's too good!

Yield: About 12 servings

6 small cooking apples
2 tbsp brown sugar
4 cups apple cider (or 3 cups cider plus 1 can of beer)
1/2 tsp nutmeg
1/2 tsp ground cinnamon
1/4 cup sugar (1/3 cup if beer is used)
2 cups medium-dry sherry
4-5 lemon slices

Early in the day:

Wash and core apples but leave whole and do not peel. Arrange in a baking pan, sprinkle with brown sugar and bake in 350 oven for about 25 minutes (or until tender but not falling apart). Set aside.

When you are ready to serve:

In a sauce pan over low-medium heat warm cider (or cider beer combination) just to boiling point. Reduce heat to warm and add nutmeg, cinnamon, sugar, sherry and lemon slices. Stir to dissolve sugar, cover and allow to steep on warm burner for about 5 minutes (don't let the mixture boil!). Pour into prewarmed punch bowl and float the baked apples in it. Keep hot on a food warmer if possible, in any case serve warm.

Welsh Cakes

These treats are a cross between English muffins and pancakes... but uniquely Welsh. They make a nice change for breakfast or brunch, easy to fix, and quite nutritious too (especially if you use all or part whole wheat flour).

Yield: About 6 cakes
Oven setting: 325 degrees Fahrenheit

   1 cup flour
   1 tsp baking powder
   1 tsp salt
   1 egg
   1/2 cup butter/margarine
   1/2 cup sugar
   1/4 tsp ground cinnamon
   1/3 cup dried currents

Combine flour, baking powder, salt and butter/margarine and blend together until the texture is crumbly. Beat the egg and add with sugar, cinnamon and currents. Mix well.

Roll out dough to about 1/4 inch thickness on a lightly floured board. Using a floured cutter, cut into 3-inch circles. Place the cakes on a lightly oiled cookie sheet, allowing at least 1/2 inch to separate one from another. Bake for 5 minutes and then turn the cakes over and bake for 5 minutes with the other side up. Serve with butter or margarine and jam.

Crispy Wheat Crackers

Crackers are not often thought of as a home-kitchen product, but there is no reason why they shouldn't be. There are lots of different crackers that you can bake yourself, (a recipe for do-it-yourself Graham Crackers is on page 81) and you'll find the taste will be infinitely better than store-bought. You'll also have the bonus of knowing exactly what these delicious snacks contain... and it won't be preservatives to extend shelf life!

Yield: About 100 crackers
Oven setting: 325 degrees Fahrenheit

> **3 tbsp butter/margarine**
> **1 1/2 cups all-purpose flour**
> **1/2 cup whole wheat flour**
> **1/2 cup sugar**
> **1/2 tsp salt**
> **1/2 cup milk** (or a little more depending on the dryness of
>   your flours)

Remove butter/margarine from refrigerator and allow to soften.

Mix both flours, sugar, and salt together in a large bowl. Using a pastry cutter (or your food processor or electric mixer), mix in the softened butter/margarine until the mixture is grainy and looks like cornmeal.

Add the milk slowly, using only enough to bind the dry ingredients together. Knead the dough for about five minutes to blend everything together and soften the gluten of the flours.

Because the crackers will be very thin, it is best to roll out only a portion of the dough at one time. Use a pastry cloth or lightly flour your cutting board or counter. Roll the dough very thin, not more than 1/8th inch thick and thinner than that is even better. (A pastry cloth cover for your rolling pin will help keep the dough from sticking to it.) Trim the sides of the rolled out dough to make a rectangle and then cut the rectangle into 1 1/2 to 2-inch squares.

Place the squares on a cookie sheet (they can be close but should not touch). Sprinkle very lightly with salt if you like and then, using a fork, prick each cracker two or three times.

Bake for about 20 minutes or until golden brown. Cool on a rack.

White Sauce Mix

There certainly is nothing uncommon about white sauce, but this simple mix probably does not have the popularity it deserves considering how convenient it is to have on hand. Keep it in your refrigerator to make creamed soups, cheese sauce (just add the cheese), souffle bases, and myriad other things at mealtime.

Yield: 3 cups of sauce mix

2 cups nonfat dry milk
1 cup all-purpose flour
1 tsp salt
1 cup soft butter/margarine

In a large bowl combine dry milk, flour and salt. Mix well. With pastry blender or using your mixer or food processor, cut in the butter/margarine until it forms fine crumbs. Put in an air-tight container and store in the refrigerator. Use within about a month. Makes 4 cups of mix.

To make a low-calorie version:

Use two packets of a butter substitute made of milk solids (*Butter Buds* for example) instead of butter or margarine. This version may be stored at room temperature.

Making Sauces

To Make Basic White Sauce:

For each cup of cool water:

Add 1/4 cup of the mix to make a thin white sauce (for creamed soups, for instance).

Add 1/2 cup mix to make a medium thick white sauce (for sauce on vegetables, for instance).

Add 3/4 cup mix to make a thick white sauce (to use in souffle, for instance).

To Make Cheese Sauce:

Make cheese sauce by adding 1/2 to 1 cup shredded cheese to 1 cups of warm sauce and stirring until melted and well mixed.

To Make Curry Sauce:

Make curry sauce by adding 1 tsp that has been heated for a few moments in a little oil to 1 cup of prepared white sauce.

White Winter Vegetable Puree

Mashed potatoes are good, but mashed potatoes combined with other white vegetables are great. This is a good chance to introduce some vegetables that might not win a popularity contest on their own such as turnips and celeriac.

Yield: 6 servings

1/2 pound turnips
1/2 pound parsnips
1/2 pound celeriac
1/2 pound potatoes
1 1/2 tsp salt
2 tbsp butter/margarine
Paprika

Peel and chop vegetables. Cook until tender in boiling water or steamer. About 15 minutes. Drain if cooked in water and puree in blender, food processor or using vegetable masher. Mound in serving bowl, place butter/margarine in center and dust with paprika.

Wine Gelatin

These attractive food accessories may be used either alone as an appetizer before the meal perhaps served with melba toast or a rich cracker, or they may be used as part of the entree particularly for a cool summer supper.

Yield: 4 servings

> **1 envelope unflavored gelatin**
> **1/2 cup cold water**
> **1/2 tsp salt**
> **1 tsp sugar**
> **1 tbsp lemon juice**
> **1 1/2 cups wine** (see below for suggestions)
> **Other ingredients as appropriate** (see below for suggestions)

In a small pan add gelatin to water and stir. Allow gelatin to soften for 2 minutes then place on low heat and warm stirring constantly for 2 to 3 minutes or until granules are completely dissolved. Remove from heat and add salt, sugar, lemon juice and wine. Add other ingredients (see below for suggestions) and pour into mold or individual molds. Chill until set.

Suggestions for serving:

Use a dry white wine such as chablis or chenin blanc. Just before gelatin sets completely, stir in 1 cup cooked and cleaned small shrimp, or 1/2 chopped avocado and 1/2 cup chopped water chestnuts.

Use a rose or blush wine. Just before gelatin sets completely, stir in 1 cup chopped tart apples or 1 cup chopped honey dew melon.

Use a full-bodied red wine such as merlot or zinfandel. Just before gelatin sets completely, stir in 1 cup drained shredded or diced pickled beets.

Wine Jelly

Wine jelly can be made from any kind of wine, but particularly good results can be found in using a rich mellow red such as a ruby port or for more vigorous flavor a full-bodied red table wine such as zinfandel or merlot. Rose and blush wines work well as do the fruitier whites such as riesling or gewertztraminer.

Wines made from fruits other than grapes can also be made into excellent jellies.

Wine jelly makes an unusual and appreciated gift to a dinner hostess in addition to being a welcome treat for your own table.

Yield: About 4 half pint jars

**1 3/4 cup wine
3 cups sugar
3 ounces liquid pectin
Paraffin**

Mix wine and sugar in top of double boiler. Cook over boiling water for about 5 minutes (sugar should be completely dissolved). Remove from heat and stir in pectin. Skim and immediately pour into sterilized jelly jars. Cover with thin layer of melted paraffin. Store in cool dry place.

Winter Custard

Sometimes you would like to have a simple but flavorful dessert... this is one. The whipping cream gives it some extra richness, but it is not heavy. The orange zest and juice sharpen the flavor.

Yield: 6 servings
Oven setting: 325 degrees Fahrenheit

1 1/4 cups milk
1/2 cup whipping cream
1/4 cup orange juice
6 egg yolks at room temperature
1/3 cup sugar
1/4 cup almond extract
1 tsp finely grated orange zest
Nutmeg, freshly grated if possible

Combine the milk, cream, and orange juice in a small saucepan and bring to a low simmer temperature (don't allow it to boil). In a bowl, beat the yolks until they are well blended but not frothy then mix in sugar, almond extract, and orange zest. Very slowly stir the heated milk mixture into the egg mixture.

Pour into 6 individual custard cups. Dust tops with nutmeg and place the cups in a large baking pan. Pour about 1-inch of hot water into the baking pan and bake for about 30 minutes or until no custard sticks to a knife inserted into the center of one of the cups. Cool for 15 minutes at room temperature and then refrigerate for at least 2 hours before serving.

To serve, run a knife around the inside of the cups and turn the custards upside-down in serving dishes. Top with a little grenadine or berry syrup if you like.

Winter Jam

It's a cold winter morning and you would like to spend some time in the kitchen doing something other than meal preparation... here's just the thing. Easy to do, pretty to serve, and delicious too. Serve with a batch of biscuits hot out of the oven and you'll win all sorts of compliments.

Yield: About 6 half pint jars

About 2 pounds winter pears (Bosc, Anjou or other firm
   pear)
1 large orange
3/4 cup canned crushed pineapple well drained
1/4 cup chopped maraschino cherries
1/4 cup lemon juice
1 pkg powdered pectin
5 cups sugar

(See "Canning Using a Boiling Water Bath Process" on page 29 for complete information on how to process the Winter Jam for long-term storage.)

Pare pears, remove cores, stems and seeds and grind (You need to have 3 cups ground pears). Peel orange, remove seeds and grind. In a large pan (8 quarts or more capacity), mix fruit and lemon juice. Stir in pectin. Place over high heat and rapidly bring to a boil while you stir constantly. (This should be a full rolling boil that you cannot stir down.)

Add sugar all at once, continue stirring constantly and again bring to a full rolling boil. Continue to boil for exactly one minute and then immediately remove from heat. Let the jam rest for about 10 minutes then skim foam from top and stir the fruit to distribute it evenly.

Fill and seal prepared half pint jars and process in boiling water bath for 5 minutes. (See page 29.)

Yellow Winter Vegetable Puree

Here is a vegetable casserole that is not only pretty to look at, but good for you too... a lot of vitamin A in this one! A nice addition to fall and winter dinner tables. You can make it up in advance too and reheat to serve.

Yield: 6 servings

3/4 pound carrots
1/2 pound sweet potatoes
1/2 pound rutabaga
1 1/2 tsp salt
2 tbsp butter/margarine
Nutmeg to taste

Peel and chop vegetables. Cook in boiling water or steam until tender. Drain if cooked in water and puree either in blender or food process or with vegetable masher until smooth. Stir in salt. Mound in serving dish, place butter/margarine in the center and dust with nutmeg.

Zucchini Bread

What... another Zucchini Bread recipe? Only because most zucchini bread recipes aren't really very good, they are too heavy, too moist, and just plain gummy to eat. This one is none of those things and so is included not because the idea of zucchini bread is uncommon, but because good zucchini bread recipes are.

Yield: 2 8x5-inch loaves
Oven setting: 350 degrees Fahrenheit

- **3 cups all-purpose flour**
- **1 tsp salt**
- **1 tsp baking soda**
- **1 tsp baking powder**
- **2 tsp ground cinnamon**
- **1 tsp ground mace**
- **1 cup finely chopped nuts**
- **3 eggs**
- **1 1/4 cup sugar**
- **1 cup oil** (corn or sunflower)
- **2 tsp vanilla extract**
- **2 cups grated zucchini** (use small to medium sized zucchini)

Prepare two 8x5-inch loaf pans by greasing well and dusting with flour.

Combine flour, salt, baking soda, baking powder, cinnamon, mace, and chopped nuts in a small bowl and set aside.

In a slightly larger bowl, beat the eggs until light and frothy. Add sugar gradually and then add the oil. Mix well. Add the vanilla and grated zucchini. Add the rest of the dry ingredients all at once and mix only until everything is moistened.

Pour the batter into the two prepared loaf pans and bake at 350 degrees for about 1 hour. (Test for doneness by inserting a cake tester or wooden skewer in the center of the loaf, if it comes out clean, the loaf is done.)

Let the loaves remain in the pans for 10 minutes and then remove from pans and cool on cooling racks. Let the loaves cool completely before slicing. (For really thin slices, wrap in plastic and place in the refrigerator over night before slicing.) Store, wrapped in plastic wrap, in the refrigerator and use within a week. You can also wrap in foil and freeze for up to a year.

Zucchini Casserole

This delightful, light zucchini baked dish goes well with almost any kind of meat. Since zucchini is at its best during the summer, be sure to try it when you barbecue. This recipe calls for olive oil and, while it is possible to use any good cooking oil, the olive oil adds just a little extra flavor that is noticeable and welcome.

Yield: 6 generous servings
Oven setting: 350 degrees Fahrenheit

   3 eggs
   8 cups diced zucchini
   1 cup chopped green pepper
   1 cup chopped onion
   1 cup soft bread crumbs
   1 cup grated sharp Cheddar cheese
   1/2 cup olive oil
   1 tsp dried basil (or 3 tsp chopped fresh basil)
   1/2 tsp dried oregano (or 2 tsp chopped fresh oregano)
   1 tsp salt
   1/2 tsp pepper

Beat the eggs until light in color. Combine zucchini, green pepper, onion, crumbs, cheese, olive oil, basil, oregano, salt and pepper. Spoon into a buttered 13x9-inch baking dish and bake at 350 degrees Fahrenheit for 45 minutes.

Zucchini Patties

Of zucchini recipes there is no end. These oh-so-bountiful summer vegetables can be found in everything from breads to puddings. Only three are included in this collection, but they are three guaranteed-to-please recipes.

One word of advice is that you use only young, smallish, tender zucchinis when you cook. As the squashes mature, they lose their flavor which was delicate at best, and become dry and tasteless.

Yield: 4 servings

> **2 eggs**
> **3 cups shredded zucchini**
> **1 cup baking mix** (purchased or your own mix)
> **1/2 cup grated Parmesan cheese**
> **1/4 cup grated onion**
> **1/2 tsp dried oregano** (1 1/2 tsp fresh)
> **1 cup Italian-seasoned bread crumbs** (your own or commercially prepared)

Beat eggs slightly and combine with all other ingredients. Divide the batter into 8 parts and form patties. Put seasoned bread crumbs in a shallow bowl and place each patty in the crumbs to coat on both sides. Heat olive oil in a large skillet and saute the patties on both sides. Serve immediately.

In Conclusion....

Why do things sometimes go wrong?

Most of us who cook never stop to think that as cooks we are, in fact, practicing chemists and physicists. Every time we enter the kitchen to fix something to eat, we are performing some fairly complex maneuvers that bring physics and chemistry into our lives in a very real way.

How the chemical and physical reactions of food preparation work is usually not of particular interest, even though these reactions are often at the bottom of what goes wrong when we cook. What we really want is to cook things that look and taste good. We want food that everyone will enjoy eating whether it is pizza, scrambled eggs or a standing rib roast.

What follows is a list of some of the reasons our best efforts don't always bring forth something that is exactly what we would like it to be. However, before starting that list, there are a few things all of us should keep in mind.

Don't be unduly upset if a dish isn't absolutely perfect or doesn't look exactly like a photograph in a magazine.
If you care about what you cook, each time you prepare a dish you will gain experience and become more confident, and confidence is 90% of success. The important question is, how does it taste?

Don't be so afraid of failure that you miss the fun of experimenting.
With very few exceptions, most recipes do not have to be followed slavishly. After you have been cooking for a while you realize, somewhat to your surprise, that you can "go it alone" and use recipes for ideas and inspiration as well as following them exactly.

While on the subject of recipes, let's not forget that sometimes a recipe can simply be wrong.
This can be particularly true of recipes that are printed in newspapers where they are sometimes taken off the wire service and printed without careful editing. Read recipes through before you start and see if the directions and ingredients called for make sense to you.

Be cautious when you double or halve recipes.
Some recipes simply don't lend themselves to changes in quantity. This is particularly true when you make jams and jellies, for instance.

Learn from your mistakes.
Here's an example: if you use a pan smaller than the one that is called for

in the recipe to bake a cake layer but bake it the called for length of time indicated, you will probably find that the cake has not cooked in the center. Next time simply either use a larger pan or bake the cake longer.

Be aware that every cook, from the television chef to the person who is just starting out, has failures in the kitchen. Somehow everyone survives, and so will you.

Having said that, let's look at some of the things that can go wrong and why...

BISCUITS

...are not flaky

Oil was substituted for shortening. (You need to have the tiny "lumps" of shortening to make the product flaky and tender. Oil blends into the mixture totally and causes the batter to be gummy and the biscuit to be firm. For very best results, the shortening should be cold.)

Dough was mixed too much. (Only mix until all of the dry ingredients have been moistened.)

...are dry and crumbly.

Too much flour and/or too little liquid was used. (Flour dries as it ages and so flour that has been on the shelf for some time will take up more moisture than flour more freshly milled. Only the cook can tell when the proportions are just right. This is more often a problem with dropped biscuits than with rolled biscuits, because the latter have the gluten in the flour slightly softened during the kneading and rolling procedures.)

The biscuits have become cold. (Try warming them up before serving, often that is all that is necessary to solve the problem of crumbling.)

...are tough.

Too little shortening was used. (You may want to cut calories by cutting down on fat used but this is a place that doing so can cause problems.)

Dough was mixed too much. (Mix only until dry ingredients are well moistened.)

Too much flour was used. (Be careful about the amount of flour you use when rolling the biscuits out, a surprising amount can be added at that point and that additional flour can cause problems.)

...are heavy.

Too much shortening can cause this, as can inadequate baking time.

...are mis-shaped.

Dough should be the same thickness throughout. (Pat out evenly, push the outer edges of the dough toward the center to level it before starting to cut the biscuits.)

Cut biscuits by pressing the cutter straight down through the dough. (If the cutter is twisted as it cuts, the result will be a rough edge and possibly a mis-shaped biscuit as well.)

BREAD MADE WITH BAKING POWDER (Quick Bread)

...has a crack down the middle of the loaf.

This is just what it should have...no mistake at all! (If the top is simply rounded, or flat, the batter has been over-mixed. Mix only until the dry ingredients have been well moistened.)

...is dry and crumbly.

Too much flour has been used and flour was not adequately mixed into the batter. (Batter should spread smoothly into the pan.)

Bread has baked too long. (Use a cake tester and probe the center of the loaf. If it comes out clean, the bread is done. Also gently press the center of the loaf, you should feel resistance and no stickiness.)

...is tough and gummy.

Too much liquid has been used. (Zucchini breads are particularly a problem in this area because the amount of moisture in the zucchini can vary greatly. Adjust the amount of liquid you use to accommodate for extra juicy zucchinis!)

Not enough shortening was used. (Adequate shortening is needed to make the dough tender.)

Too much flour. (If the proportion of flour to liquid and shortening is not right, the loaf will be tough.)

The batter was mixed too much. (As with any batter that uses baking powder as leavening, mix only until the dry ingredients are moistened.)

...is too moist and crumbly, falls apart.

Too much liquid was used. (You should have to scoop the batter into the pan, it should not be so thin that it will pour.)

Cut while still warm. (Allow quick breads to cool completely before cutting. This allows the moisture to distribute itself evenly throughout the loaf and will also allow the flavors to mellow. Ideally, quick breads should be baked one day and served the next. Use a sharp knife for slicing, especially if the bread contains chopped nuts.)

...streusel topping sinks into the batter.

Topping had chunks that were too large. (Mix the topping with your fingers until it is uniform in size, something like very coarse cornmeal, then distribute it as evenly as possible over the top of the batter. If you use nuts, chop them into very small pieces.)

BREAD MADE WITH YEAST

...did not rise enough before baking.

The yeast was out-dated. (Yeast has a limited shelf-life and should be used before the expiration date printed on it. If it is too old, it simply is not lively enough to do the job.)

The yeast has been stored in a warm, humid environment. (Yeast is best stored where it is cool and dry. That usually means that it should not be stored too near the stove. If you store it in the refrigerator, allow it to warm to room temperature before using.)

The liquid was too hot when added and so "killed" the yeast. (Liquids should be between 95 and 105 degrees Fahrenheit.)

The dough was too cool while it was rising. (Dough should be kept at about 85 degrees Fahrenheit to raise properly.)

The dough was not kneaded enough. (Dough should be kneaded at least 10 minutes after all the flour has been added to soften the gluten in the flour. It will feel resilient, not heavy, when it is adequately kneaded.)

An inadequate amount of gluten in the dough. (Gluten is the part of the flour that stretches to allow dough to raise. Hard wheat has a higher proportion of gluten. "Bread Flour" is made with hard wheat and that is why bread flour is preferable to all-purpose flour when making breads. Whole grain flours are relatively low in gluten and so recipes based on whole grains will often call for the addition of white flour so that the dough raises more satisfactorily. A bread made exclusively of whole-grain flour can have an excellent flavor, but will just not raise as high.)

You have added ingredients that change the proportions of the recipe. (Adding wheat germ, soy flour, and other healthful ingredients is a good idea, but can disrupt the balance and prevent the dough from raising. Either find a recipe that calls for those ingredients and follow it, or experiment with your own recipe until you find the amount of additional ingredients that can be added without causing a problem. A rule-of-thumb is that you may usually substitute about 1/4 cup of an alternate ingredient per cup of flour, for instance 3/4 cup flour plus 1/4 cup wheat germ equals one cup.)

...did not rise enough as it was baking.

The dough temperature during the initial raising period was too high. (Should be about 85 degrees Fahrenheit for best results.)

The dough was allowed to rise too long before baking. (Dough should roughly double in size before baking. Raising completes in the heat of the oven.)

The oven was not hot enough. (Bread needs the heat of the oven for the final expansion of gases that complete the raising process. An oven thermometer is an excellent investment. Use it to check your oven thermostat to make sure that when you call for 400 degrees, you are actually getting that temperature in your oven.)

Bread that sinks in the middle while it bakes was not kneaded enough. (Knead for about 10 minutes after ingredients have been mixed thoroughly. Dough should be resilient and feel "alive".)

...has tough, lumpy sections in the middle.

You have added too much liquid. (The dough was simply too wet to bake properly.)

The dough may not have been mixed enough before you started kneading. (It is important that all of the ingredients are well blended before the kneading starts.)

The dough was not adequately kneaded. (The gluten needs to be softened and distributed throughout the dough otherwise some parts of the dough will rise more than others.)

The dough was too tightly rolled. (If you roll the dough to form the loaf, the center part should not be rolled so tightly that it pinches together. There needs to be a little expansion space for the dough to raise.)

Dough was torn into sections to form loaves instead of cutting with a sawing motion. (By tearing the original dough in halves or thirds to make loaves, the gluten fibers can be damaged.)

...the loaf top is not rounded and has browned unevenly.

If the loaf is too tall, the baking pan may have been to small. (The dough has risen the expected amount, but in the smaller pan has no place to go but up.)

If the loaf has a high spot in the center, the oven was too hot. (The outside of the loaf baked too fast and forced the unbaked portion up in the center.)

Uneven browning can be caused by too many loaves being baked at one time or a single loaf being baked away from the center of the oven. (Distribute the loaves in the oven so the heat can circulate adequately.)

If the top of the loaf doesn't brown, the pan is probably too big. (The dough needs to rise high enough that the top is directly exposed to the dry heat of the oven.)

...the top of the loaves crack. (Not to be confused with the "gash" that is deliberately cut in breads such as French bread.)

Too much flour was used in the kneading process. (Only add as much as you need to keep the dough from being sticky. The dough should not be crumbly with flour.)

The dough was inadequately kneaded. (It takes about ten minutes of vigorous kneading to adequately distribute and soften the gluten.)

The baked loaf was cooled in a draft or otherwise cooled too quickly. (The outside becomes cool while the inside is still hot.)

...the loaves are unequal in size and so bake unevenly.

Different amounts of dough were used for individual loaves. (If you have a kitchen scale, weigh the dough before putting the loaf-shaped pieces into the pan. They should be within an ounce or so in weight. Estimating by eye can be deceiving.)

...the bread is soggy on the bottom.

The bread was cooled in the pan instead of on a cooling rack. (The bread pan cools faster than the bread so that the warmth of the bread can produce "steam" on the inside of the pan. That moisture is then reabsorbed by the bread causing the crust to be moist and soggy.

The bread should not be wrapped until it has cooled to room temperature. (The same thing happens here, the warm bread condenses moisture against the inside of the wrapping and that moisture is reabsorbed.)

...crust is too thick.

Baked in a pan that tends to produce a thicker crust. (Glass pans in particular can cause a thicker crust to form. Incidentally, if a glass bread pan is used, be sure to reduce the oven temperature about 25 degrees below the temperature called for in the recipe.)

...texture is not right.

Tough bread is usually caused by too much flour in the dough. (Use no more than is called for to make the dough easy to handle and be particularly careful while adding flour during the kneading process that too much is not added.)

Loaves that are dry and crumbly are caused by using too much flour, by inadequate kneading, and by raising too long before baking.

"Heavy" loaves can be caused by using too much flour, by not having enough gluten available (because proportionally too much whole grain flour is used), or because the dough was not allowed to raise long enough.

Coarse grain in a loaf of bread can be caused by using too much yeast, inadequate raising time or by the temperature of the oven being too low.

Holes in the loaf can be caused by the dough being kneaded too much, being allowed to raise too long before baking or if the temperature when the dough raises is too warm, or air pockets being formed as the loaves were shaped.

...sticks to pan.

Not enough fat content in dough to prevent sticking. (This sometimes happens when making French or Italian breads that do not contain oil. It can be prevented by sprinkling the baking sheet with cornmeal.)

CAKE

...does not rise properly.

Ingredients were not thoroughly mixed. (It is important to mix shortening, butter, or margarine and sugar together completely, this process is called "creaming". It is also important that eggs are beaten in thoroughly before pouring the batter into the pan.)

Baking pan used was too large. (The batter is simply spread out over too large an area.)

The oven was not preheated. (Cake batter, like other baked goods leavened with baking powder, needs the immediate heat of the oven to cause gas expansion that makes the cake rise as it bakes.)

Not enough leavening was used. (Be sure to follow directions, it is possible to mis-read a recipe and use a teaspoonful of an ingredient when a tablespoon is actually called for.)

Not baked long enough. (Uncooked batter in the center of the cake can result in the whole cake being flat and heavy.)

Egg whites were over-beaten before folding in. (In recipes that call for the eggs to be separated and the whites beaten before folding in, beat the whites only until they will hold a peak. If beaten until dry, they will not hold the air pockets that help the cake to rise.)

Too much shortening, butter, or margarine. (The proportion of the leavening agent, usually baking powder, to shortening is not adequate to allow adequate rising.)

...sinks in the center.

Oven was too cool and center of cake has not completely baked in the indicated time. (Use an oven thermometer to check the oven setting and make sure oven is actually reaching the temperature called for.)

Pan was too small. (If the pan is too full, the batter does not become completely baked in the amount of time indicated in the recipe. Either use the pan size called for or adjust the baking time to allow more time for the thicker amount of batter.)

...bakes higher on one side than the other.

Oven is uneven. (Place a carpenter's level on the center shelf of the oven and see if it is level. Most stoves have adjusting devices on the bottom that can be used to make them level if that is the problem.)

...has cracks.

In the top, cracks are caused by baking in an oven that is too hot. (The top of the cake bakes while the center is still in batter form. As the internal batter rises, it forces its way out through the top of the cake.)

In the bottom, cracks are usually caused by removing the cake from the pan too quickly. (Allow the cake to cool in the pan for about 10 minutes before turning out onto a cake cooling rack. If the cake doesn't tip out easily, place the pan on a wet towel for five minutes, the condensation that forms between the warm cake and the cool pan will sometimes make it easier to turn the cake out.)

Too much flour. (If the batter is too dry, it may simply part because of lack of adhesion. Batters should be thick but still pourable before baking.)

...has tunnels.

Air pockets were baked into the cake. (Before placing the filled pans in the oven, drop each one from about six inches onto the counter top. This will dislodge air bubbles caught in the batter and cause the bubbles to rise to the top.)

Too many eggs, or eggs that were too large, were used. (Most recipes are based on using the egg size designated as "large". A "large" egg weighs about two ounces. When extra large are used the effect is to change the proportions of the recipe.)

Batter was not mixed enough. (It is important that all of the ingredients are mixed together and that the batter is smooth before pouring it into the pans.)

...is tough, coarse and/or grainy.

Batter has been over-mixed. (Like all baked goods using baking powder, cakes should be mixed only until the batter is smooth. There is a fine line between under- and over-mixing. Usually about 4 minutes with a mixer or 300 strokes by hand should do the job, but follow recipe directions.)

Too much flour. (Measure with reasonable care, remember that batter should still be pourable, not so thick that it must be scooped out of the bowl.)

...is gummy.

Too much liquid. (Batter should not be runny. If you do add too much liquid, don't try to save the situation by adding more flour because you will disrupt the proportions. It's better just to start over.)

Too much shortening, butter, margarine. (Again, it's the proportions among the ingredients that is important. A certain amount of baking powder will cause a certain proportion of other ingredients to turn into a cake that rises nicely and has a good texture. If any of those ingredients are noticeably changed, the result is not good.)

Substitution of honey for sugar. (It's a popular idea that honey can be substituted for sugar on a one-for-one basis. Unfortunately there are aspects to honey other than its sweetness. Foremost among these is the liquid that it adds to the mixture.)

Cake has cooled in pan. (Some cakes are cooled and frosted in the pan, but most are turned out onto a cake rack to cool. This allows the bottom to "dry out". If the cake is left in the pan, the pan cools before the cake which causes a layer of moisture to form between the cake and the pan. If the cake is not removed from the pan, this condensate can be absorbed into the bottom of the cake and will cause it to be soggy and gummy.)

...has a sticky top.

Not baked long enough. (The cake simply is not completely cooked.)

Cake was baked in a microwave oven. (While the microwave will "cook" the cake, the exterior does not achieve the firm quality of a cake baked in a conventional oven.)

Too much liquid was used. (Batter should be smooth and pourable, but not runny.)

Oven was not hot enough. (Check your oven thermometer to make sure the temperature set on the thermostat is being reached inside the oven.)

There was a lot of humidity in the air. (Weather can have an effect on all baked goods.)

...sticks to the pan and is hard to remove.

Can be caused by using butter, margarine, or liquid oil instead of shortening to grease the pan. (Use a generous amount of shortening and make sure you spread it all over the bottom and sides of the pan. Dust with flour, tip excess flour out of pan before adding batter.)

CANDY

Most problems with candy making can be traced to the temperature and humidity of the kitchen. Candy will be turn out best if your kitchen is under 70 degrees Fahrenheit (65-68 degrees is ideal), if the day is not humid, if there is not a lot of steam being generated by other things cooking, and if there are no drafts in the kitchen.

Other problems with candy are also temperature related... use a candy thermometer to be really sure you have cooked it enough. There are a lot of other ways suggested to test doneness (dropping into cold water, and so forth) but the only truly reliable way is to use a thermometer.

CHICKEN (and other poultry)

Broiled chicken

...cooked on the outside but not in the center.

Chicken pieces were placed too near the heat source. (The thicker the pieces, the further away from the heat source it should be. This is because it simply takes time for the heat to penetrate into the center of the piece.)

...tough and dry after cooking.

Over-cooking, or using a chicken other than a fryer/broiler can cause this. (If this happens, you can sometimes save the situation by serving the chicken with a sauce.)

Fried chicken

...greasy.

Temperature of oil is too low. (The oil should be hot enough to seal the outside of the chicken piece by cooking it quickly so that additional oil does not penetrate the meat.)

...not browned.

Caused by putting too many chicken pieces into the fryer at one time. (Adding too many pieces at one time lowers the temperature of the oil which slows browning and "sealing" of the chicken pieces. The pieces do not brown nicely and are often greasy as well.)

...browned on the outside but not adequately cooked throughout.

Caused by oil temperature being too hot. (Heat the oil until you can just get a whiff of the "hot oil" odor then add the chicken. After pieces have lightly browned, reduce the heat to finish the cooking process.)

...coating falls off chicken pieces.

Each piece must be dried thoroughly before coating. (Try the Batter for Deep Fried Foods recipe for a batter that will work well when you like a batter-dipped piece. For breading, cover each piece with flour, then dip in beaten egg, and then in seasoned crumbs and allow the coating to "set" for about an hour before cooking.)

Roasted chicken (or other poultry)

...tough and dry.

Over-cooked. (Use a meat thermometer to check internal temperature. If a meat thermometer is not used, be sure you use the correct weight of the bird when estimating baking time. Roasting in foil will decrease cooking time.)

Under-cooked. (Poultry can also be tough if it is not cooked enough, but it will not be dry and will not come from the bone easily.)

CHOCOLATE

...separates when melted.

Melted over too hot a heat source. (If you are melting a large amount of chocolate it is best melted over simmering water in the top of a double boiler. For smaller amounts, chocolate can be melted in a microwave [follow manufacturer's instructions, or use a medium to low setting], or in a measuring cup over simmering water.)

...acquires a whitish-coating.

This is called a "bloom" and happens when chocolate has been stored in a warm place. (The chocolate is quite safe to use and the flavor will not be affected.)

...becomes "stiff" when melted.

If any moisture gets into the melting chocolate, this can happen. (To get things back to normal, simply beat in a teaspoon of shortening for every ounce of chocolate melted. Do not use butter in this instance because it contains enough liquid that it will make the matter worse not better.)

COOKIES

...spread out too much.

Too much liquid in the dough. (In addition to ingredients commonly thought of as "liquid", this can also be caused by using eggs that are too large because eggs provide a certain amount of liquid to the recipe.)

Butter used instead of shortening. (Butter contains more water than shortening and so makes the dough more moist. Butter cookie recipes allow for this difference but other recipes may not.)

Cookie sheet was over-greased. (With most cookies little if any grease is needed on the cookie sheet to keep the cookies from sticking.)

Oven not hot enough. (The cookies did not "set up" quickly in the oven. Check setting against an oven thermometer to make sure your oven is heating adequately.)

Cookie sheet is warm. (Let the pan cool off a bit between batches so that the shortening in the cookies does not melt as it come in contact with the metal of the baking pan.)

...brown on the bottom but not cooked on top.

Cookie sheet is too dark. (Light, silvery pans are usually best for cookies because dark pans absorb heat and transfer it to the cookie dough faster than the heat in the oven can cook the top portion.)

Too much sugar used. (The sugar browns quickly where it rests against the hot metal of the cookie sheet.)

Baked too low in the oven. (If you are baking more than one sheet of cookies at a time, be sure the bottom sheet is well up in the oven, also stagger the sheets so that there is room for the heat to circulate.)

...brown on top but not cooked on the bottom.

Bottom heat is blocked by another cookie sheet being placed directly below.

Broiler is turning on. (Over is set for pre-heat or broil instead of bake.)

...some cook faster than others.

Cookie sizes vary. (Try to keep cookies as uniform in size and shape as possible so that they will cook in the same time period.)

Cookie sheet too large for oven. (Outer cookies will cook first. Either use a smaller sheet, or simply remove the cookies as they are baked and return the sheet for the rest to finish.)

...are gummy

Not baked long enough. (Check the oven temperature with a thermometer, it may not be reaching the temperature set on the thermostat.)

Cooled on the cookie sheet instead of a rack. (As in cakes, the metal cools before the cookie and a layer of steam condenses between them. As it cools, the moisture is absorbed into the bottom of the cookie.)

Cool bar cookies completely before cutting (unless recipe recommends otherwise) so that cut edges do not clump together as you cut them.

...are hard and dry.

Baked too long at too low a temperature. (You want to bake the cookie, not dry it out.)

Too much flour was used. (Cookie dough should be firm but not stiff. When cutting out rolled cookies, consider using a dusting of powdered sugar instead of flour on the board, it will cut down on the flour necessary but you do have to watch to make sure the cookies do not brown too quickly because of the extra sugar.)

Not enough liquid was used, eggs were too small. (Usually large-size eggs are recommended for most recipes unless otherwise indicated.)

CREAM

...will not whip.

Not high enough fat content. (To whip properly, cream must be at least 30% fat or higher. It is the fat that gives it stability.)

Cream is too warm. (If too warm, fat will "melt" and not be firm. For best results, chill not only the cream but also the beaters and bowl you are going to use. If the room is warm, place the bowl holding the cream into a larger bowl containing iced water.)

...turns to butter.

You've gone a bit to far. Stop whipping when the cream is firm enough to hold a peak when you remove the beater. Beyond that you run the risk of butter forming, and it can happen very quickly. Once turned into butter there is no way to reverse things.

...curdles when used in a cooked dish.

Temperature too high. (Because of the high fat content, cream reacts quickly to heat. Cook slowly and at a low temperature, preferably over simmering water in a double boiler.)

Too much acid in the dish. (The fat content also makes dishes containing cream susceptible to curdling in the presence of acid such as you might find in citrus fruits or tomatoes. These dishes should always be cooked in a double boiler.)

CREAM PUFFS

...did not rise adequately.

The flour-liquid mixture was over-cooked. (Cook only until the dough will leave the sides of the pan and form a ball.)

The batter was under-beaten. (Ingredients must be well blended.)

The balls of dough were flattened or not large enough when formed. (Balls should be nicely mounded and close to the size you want in the finished product.)

Too much liquid in dough. (Dough should be firm enough to mound and not sag.)

Not enough heat in the oven. (It is important that the oven be at the temperature called for. Check oven temperature with an oven thermometer and adjust setting if necessary.)

Simply not baked enough. (Cream puffs should be golden brown in color and firm to the touch. If in doubt, leave them in the oven for an additional 5 or 10 minutes.)

...soggy inside.

Not cooked enough. (Cream puffs need to brown on the outside, but also need to "dry out" on the inside so that they will part easily to receive the filling.)

Steam was not allowed to escape from baked cream puff. (Be sure to cut a slit in each cream puff. Use a sharp knife so that edges are not pressed together to become hard.)

CUSTARD

...is not firm.

Not cooked enough. (Check for doneness by inserting a thin knife into the center of the custard. If it comes out clean, the custard is done. If any egg mixture clings to the knife, the custard is not completely cooked.)

Proportion of eggs to milk was wrong. (Not enough eggs for the amount of milk. Use large eggs as most recipes are based on that size. If you use medium or small eggs, add at least one more egg yolk to the mixture before baking.)

Too much sugar. (Sugar melts as it cooks and can cause the mixture not to set up properly.)

Baked custard was stirred during cooking time. (If you want a soft custard, stir the mixture from time to time as it cooks. If you want a firm custard, leave it alone until you test for doneness. For an extra firm custard add more eggs.)

DRIED BEANS

...are tough and hard even after cooking.

Not cooked enough. (The length of time required to cook beans depends on the age of the beans...the older they are they longer it takes because they have continued to dry out as they age. Always pre-soak beans to minimize cooking time.)

Salt was added to cooking water. (Do not add salt to beans until they are tender because they will not soften any further after salt is added. Incidentally, you can use this information to stop beans from becoming mushy by adding salt when the beans are tender to your taste.)

Partially cooked beans have been added to an acidic mixture to finish cooking. (Acid does the same thing salt does, causes the cell wall of the bean to become less permeable and therefore water cannot penetrate to soften further. This can happen when you add partially cooked beans to a tomato-based vegetable soup or casserole dish containing tomatoes.)

...are indigestible.

Some people find beans hard to deal with for many reasons most of which are related to their digestive system.

There is a complex carbohydrate in beans that cannot be completely digested by the enzymes available in human digestive systems. In the lower digestive tract the compound is processed by our resident bacteria and in doing so various gases are given off.

The good news is that this can be avoided. Simply pre-soak the beans in warm water (2 quarts of water to each cup of beans) for four hours and pour off the soaking water. Cook the beans in 2 quarts of fresh water and discard the cooking water. Then use the beans. It might seem that you would lose a lot of nutrients by doing this, but in fact there is only a modest amount of the water-soluble B-complex vitamins and some of the amino acids (proteins) that are lost.

Rinse commercially canned beans in clear water before using.

DUMPLINGS

...are too heavy.

Lid was removed too soon. (It is important to leave the lid on so that the dumplings will raise properly.)

Dumplings are too close together in the pan. (Dumplings have to have room to expand, use a larger pan next time.)

...batter sticks to spoon.

Dip the spoon in cold water each time you put the ball of dumpling batter into the stock.

... break up in the stock

Stock is boiling too hard. (Stock should just simmer to cook the dumplings.)

EGGS

...do not separate easily.

Separate eggs while they are still cold. (The rule of thumb is that egg whites will separate from the yolk best when the egg is cold, but will beat to the highest peaks when the whites are at room temperature.)

...when cooked seem tough and rubbery.

Eggs are over-cooked. (No matter how you cook eggs, use a moderate temperature and cook only until done to your taste. Longer cooking causes the protein in the white to become tough.)

Fried eggs

...burn around edges.

Pan is too hot. (Reduce heat after egg is added.)

...tops will not set.

Not enough heat being conducted to the yolk. (Cover pan to steam the tops or baste with oil as you cook.)

...yolks break when egg is broken into pan.

Don't break the egg or eggs directly into the pan. (Break egg into shallow dish and slide the egg or eggs into the pan.)

Hard-cooked eggs

...egg shells crack.

Cold eggs were placed in very hot water. (Start cold eggs off in cold water, not warm. Pierce shell with a pin to allow gases to escape.)

...eggs are hard to peel.

Eggs were too fresh. (Hard to believe that eggs could ever be too fresh, but for hard cooked eggs slightly not-so-fresh eggs are best they have less adhesion between the shell and the white. Also cool eggs thoroughly before starting to remove the shell.)

Here's how to remove shells quickly and smoothly: Drain the hot water from the cooked eggs and vigorously shake the pan so that the shells crack from colliding with the sides of thepan. Dump the eggs into a bowl of iced water that you haveready and cool completely. The shells will slip right off.

...greenish-colored layer forms around yolk.

Egg has been cooked at too high a temperature or for too long. (It can also develop if the cooked egg is stored for a while before eating. It is harmless, although certainly not too attractive.)

Omelet

...sticks to pan.

Not enough oil was used. (Oil should be adequate to flow around the omelet pan.)

Unclarified butter was used. (Use oil or clarified butter, not butter or margarine so that the oil can be heated without burning.)

Omelet was allowed to set up before starting to move it in the pan. (Start to move the egg mixture very quickly after it has been poured into the pan.)

...becomes scrambled eggs instead of an omelet.

Eggs were stirred while being cooked. (Instead of stirring, move the eggs gently in the pan and lift the cooked portions to allow liquid egg mixture to flow under the cooked layer and reach the bottom of the pan.)

...will not turn out of the pan easily.

A straight-sided skillet has been used. (Sometimes a special pan is worth the investment. An omelet pan falls into that category. If you like omelets, purchase a curved-side omelet pan and you will find that omelets will be much more cooperative.)

Poached eggs

...stick to pan.

Poaching pan was not oiled before water was added. (This applies only if you use a "mold" in which to poach eggs either in your microwave or in boiling water, be sure to oil it well so that the egg does not stick.)

...lose shape while cooking.

Water was boiling instead of simmering and had not been acidulated. (If you poach eggs directly in simmering water, add a little lemon juice or vinegar to the water and the egg white will maintain a nice oval shape.)

...yolks break.

Eggs were broken directly into the water. (Break them into a shallow dish and slide them into the water one by one.)

Scrambled eggs

...dry and tough.

Over-cooked at too high a temperature. (Beating about a tablespoon of cold water into eggs before cooking to keep the scrambled eggs tender.)

Souffle

...does not rise properly.

Egg whites were not beaten enough. (Whites should be beaten until they hold a soft peak when the beaters are removed.)

Beaten egg whites were stirred into the sauce mixture rather than being folded in. (Gently combine the whites into the sauce using a U-shaped folding motion. Fold in only until all of the whites are blended into the mixture.)

Beaten egg whites were not added to sauce immediately after being beaten. (Beaten egg whites will loose their buoyancy as the air escapes while standing.)

Sauce mixture was not cooled before whites were folded in. (You should be able to hold the pan containing the sauce mixture on the palm of your hand without discomfort before you add the egg whites.)

...falls while it is being baked.

Oven door was opened too often or perhaps slammed shut. (Allow the souffle to bake the indicated amount of time before checking.)

...collapses before serving.

Waited too long after removing from oven to serve. (A souffle must be served almost immediately. Souffles with "body", such as spinach or broccoli souffles, will hold up longer than lighter souffles, such as those made with cheese for instance.)

...Not cooked in time indicated.

Oven temperature was too low. (Check oven temperature with an oven thermometer if there is any question about whether it reaches the called for temperature or not.)

...Browned on top but was not cooked inside.

Oven temperature was too high. (Again, an oven thermometer can potentially solve many problems. Correct oven temperatures are really very important.)

FISH

...smells "fishy"

Fish is not fresh. (Either it was not fresh when you bought it or else you have kept it too long before cooking. Don't use it.)

...falls apart after cooking.

Over-cooked. (This can happen particularly when poaching fish if it is cooked to long or cooked in boiling instead of simmering water or stock.)

...is dry and tasteless.

Over-cooked. (This usually happens when fish is broiled without being brushed with oil or margarine, or baked without any sauce or other liquid at too high a temperature. Breading helps to hold moisture in and allows you to "oven-fry" the fish.)

Fried at too high a temperature and cooked too fast. (Keep top-of-stove temperatures in the moderate range when cooking fish.)

...is tough and "stringy".

If fish was frozen before cooking, it could be from freezer "burn" caused when air was allow to be in contact with the fish while it was frozen. (Fish packages need to be tightly wrapped before freezing. If you use heavy-duty foil, be sure to press it around the fish so that there are no air pockets. Fresh caught whole fish can also be frozen in milk containers or sealable plastic bags filled with water.)

Could have been in the freezer too long before cooking. (Fish should be kept only about 6 months in the freezer.)

FLAMBE

...didn't flame.

Liquor was not warm enough to burn. (For reliable results when trying to flame a dish, be sure to warm liquor to slightly more than lukewarm, about 120 degrees Fahrenheit, before setting afire.)

Liquor was not high enough in alcohol to burn well. (You need to use at least 80 proof liquor. Wines are not high enough in alcohol to flame.)

...changed flavor of the dish.

Used too much liquor. (Use a small amount so that you don't overwhelm the flavor of the dish with the taste of the liquor.)

FRUIT, HOME-CANNED (Boiling Water Bath Method)

...syrup becomes cloudy.

May be caused by spoilage because of improper seal. It is better not to use the fruit. (Cloudy liquid can also be caused by other things such as using hard water in the syrup but it is not worth taking chances.)

...fruit floats at the top of the bottle.

Jars were not packed with enough fruit. (Pack bottles as tightly as you can without unduly bruising the fruit.)

Syrup was made with too much sugar for the fruit. (It is not necessary to use a lot of sugar in the syrup used for canning fruit. One cup of sugar to 3 cups of water, or even 1 to 4 will do the job, and also cut the calories.)

...bottle somehow loses syrup while it is being processed.

Jars were packed too full. (The metal lid should rest easily on the top of the bottle before the ring is screwed on.)

Do not unseal the bottle to add more liquid! This negates the whole purpose of processing by disturbing the seal of the lid.

...fruit darkens.

Oxidation has occurred. (Use an ascorbic or citric acid base fruit treatment to prevent darkening, or place peeled fruit into a bowl of acidulated water before packing into bottles.)

Too much "head space" has been left in the top of the bottle before processing. Leave about 1/2 inch at the top of the bottle between the fruit/syrup and the lid.

If you have other questions about preserving any kind of food at home, contact your local county extension office. They have trained home economists to help you and many publications you can consult that are a great source of information.

GARLIC

...develops a bitter taste when cooked.

Cooked at too high a heat. (Cook over heat in the moderate range of temperatures.)

Added to saute pan at the same time as onions are added. (Garlic takes less time to cook than onions, by the time the onions are cooked the garlic has cooked too much. Partially saute onions before adding garlic.)

GELATIN

...did not set up.

Too much liquid was used for the amount of gelatin. (Follow the directions on the package or in your recipe. A scant tablespoon of gelatin will jell 2 cups of liquid.)

Some ingredient prevented the gelatin from setting up. (Certain fruits such as pineapple, papayas, mangos, and figs contain an enzyme that works on the protein of the gelatin and causes it to remain soft. Use these fruits, or juices from these fruits, in the gelatin only if they are cooked.)

Gelatin was not completely dissolved. (Be sure that no grains of gelatin remain to be seen in the mixture.)

...added ingredients sink to the bottom.

Ingredients were added while gelatin was still in a liquid form. (Wait until gelatin is partially set before adding other ingredients. Mix them in carefully to distribute evenly.)

...added ingredients separate into layers.

Some added ingredients tend to rise to the top (banana slices, fresh strawberry halves, chopped nuts, and chopped apple to name a few), others tend to sink to the bottom (fresh grapes, canned fruits, and orange slices for example). You can use these tendencies to deliberately make layers in a molded gelatin if you like.)

...will not unmold easily.

Spray the mold with vegetable oil spray before adding gelatin mixture. (This will leave a "haze" on the outside of the gelatin so use only if that will not matter.)

Rinse the mold with cold water before pouring in the gelatin mixture. (This will leave a thin layer of water between the mold and the gelatin which will allow the molded gelatin to tip out more easily.)

Draw a sharp knife around the edge of the mold, place the mold on a towel wet with warm, not hot, water for a moment or two, then shake gently until you can hear it loosen in the mold. Turn out immediately. (It's a good idea to rinse the serving plate with water so that you can move the mold around without having it stick to the plate.)

...is gummy and tough.

It either has been frozen or has been left in the refrigerator too long before using. (The liquid simply evaporates over time. Use prepared gelatin within about two days for best quality.)

GRAVY

...is lumpy.

Thickener has been added directly to the hot stock. (Either mix flour with butter and cook slightly to form a roux or use uncooked ("beurre manie" or rubbed butter) and use that to thicken the gravy. Alternatively dissolve flour or cornstarch in water before adding to stock. In either case, add slowly and stir constantly as the gravy thickens.)

If lumps form anyway, use a whisk to smooth them out. (If all else fails, strain gravy through a sieve.)

...is too thin.

Not enough thickener was added. (Amount used depends on the kind of thickener used and how thick you like your gravy to be.)

Cornstarch was used as a thickener and the gravy was overcooked. (Cook cornstarch thickened mixtures only until they are thickened and then remove from heat.)

Not cooked long enough. (Flour must be cooked into the sauce before it will thicken properly.)

...tastes pasty and floury.

Not cooked enough. (Flour needs to be cooked.)

Stock was not adequately seasoned. (Deglaze the pan by adding hot stock, wine or water (or a combination) to the pan in which the meat was cooked. Carefully scrape all of the contents of the saute pan into the stock. Taste the stock before thickening and adjust the seasonings if necessary.)

HIGH ALTITUDE COOKING

Almost all recipes are developed and published to be prepared at sea level or at least at lower altitudes. For most places this is fine, but people who live at higher altitudes have a special problem than can affect just about everything they cook.

Cooks who have lived in a high altitude area for a long time are well aware of some of the changes they have to make in their cooking, but if you move from a lower altitude up to 3000 feet or more from sea level, you may be unpleasantly surprised by some of the results you have.

The basic problem is this: the higher the altitude, the lower the atmospheric pressure; the lower the atmospheric pressure, the lower the temperature at which water boils.

How that one simple fact affects what you do when you cook is quite far reaching however.

Boiling Temperature of Water

	Fahrenheit	Centigrade
Sea level	212 degrees	100 degrees
2000 feet altitude	208 degrees	98 degrees
5000 feet altitude	203 degrees	95 degrees
7000 feet altitude	198 degrees	92 degrees
10000 feet altitude	194 degrees	90 degrees
15000 feet altitude	185 degrees	85 degrees

Because water boils at a lower temperature, foods cooked in water and other liquids take longer to cook because even though the liquid may be boiling, the temperature is lower than it would be at sea level. Extend the cooking time.

If you use cornstarch to thicken a liquid, cook it over direct heat instead of in the top of a double boiler because the boiling water does not become hot enough to cook the cornstarch.

Cook milk based sauces and puddings over boiling water but cook them longer. If you cook them over direct heat they may catch and scorch.

Water and other liquids evaporate a little faster because of lower atmospheric pressure, so you have to allow a little more liquid and watch to make sure the liquid doesn't completely evaporate. (See chart below for baked products.)

Baked products raise more quickly because the gases from the leavening agent expand quickly. This can result in a finished product with a coarse texture. Use slightly less baking powder. (See chart below.)

Flour may dry out more quickly at higher altitudes.

Deep-fat fried foods will brown more quickly at higher altitudes. Decrease frying temperature. (See chart below.)

When preserving fruits, jams, jellies, and other food products that are suitable to be processed in a boiling water bath, extend the cooking time to adjust for the lower temperature of the boiling water and to allow the product to be completely heated throughout. (Check with your local county extension office's home economics agent for specific information about your location.)

High Altitude Cooking Adjustments

at 3000 feet:
    for baked products with baking powder:
      add 1-2 tbsp additional liquid and
      decrease baking powder by 1/8 tsp
    for deep fried foods:
      decrease temperature by 10 degrees
    for boiling water bath canning:
      check with your local county extension office

at 5000 feet:
    for baked products with baking powder:
      add 2-3 tbsp additional liquid and
      decrease baking powder by 1/8 tsp
    for deep fried foods:
      decrease temperature by 15 degrees
    for boiling water bath canning:
      check with your local county extension office

at 7000 feet:
    for baked products with baking powder:
      add 3-4 tbsp additional liquid and
      decrease baking powder by rounded 1/4 tsp
    for deep fried foods:
      decrease temperature by 20 degrees
    for boiling water bath canning:
      check with your local county extension office

JAM

...does not thicken and is syrupy.

Too much sugar was used. (Measure carefully and follow directions.)

Too little pectin, acid, or sugar. (Having the correct proportions among fruit, sugar, pectin, and acid are essential for success in making jams and jellies.)

...darkens at top of jar.

An imperfect seal has allowed air to come into the jar and oxidation has caused the darkening. (Do not use if mold has formed on the top of the jam.)

...color of jam fades over time.

If storage area is too warm this can happen. Excessively long storage can also cause it particularly in red fruits such as berries. (Use jams within a year for best appearance and flavor.

...fruit floats instead of being distributed throughout jar.

Pieces of fruit are too large. (Process the fruit into equal sized pieces by carefully chopping or grinding.)

Jam was not stirred before pouring into jars. (Allow jam to rest for about 5 minutes after boiling. Stir to distribute the fruit and then ladle into sterile jars.)

JELLY

...is cloudy.

Has been allowed to partially set before pouring into jars. (Pour jelly into jars while it is still liquid.)

Juice contained fruit pulp. (Strain the juice through cloth to remove all fruit pulp and fibers before starting to make jelly.)

Jelly set-up to quickly. (Often caused by using immature fruit which is higher in pectin than fruit that is fully ripened.)

...crystals form in jelly.

Crystals throughout jelly may be caused by too much sugar being used. (Be sure to measure sugar carefully and follow directions regarding the amount to use.)

Crystals formed on top of jelly caused by evaporation. (Cover jelly when stored after opening.)

...too soft.

Too much juice in mixture. (Measure juice carefully.)

Too little sugar. (The correct proportion among sugar, juice, acid, and pectin are very important to successful jelly making.)

Too little acid in the fruit. (Fruit may be over-ripe. Recipe may call for lemon juice to increase acidity.)

Too big a batch was made at one time. (Don't try to double recipes for jelly.)

...too stiff.

Overcooked. (Follow directions carefully. Use a clock or watch with a sweep second hand to accurately time the jelly's cooking time after all ingredients have been added.)

Too much pectin. (If adding pectin, use only the amount called for. Be aware that immature fruit contains more pectin than fully-ripened fruit.)

Not enough juice. (If you don't have quite enough juice to meet the requirements of the recipe, you can add a little water to bring the quantity up to the correct amount.)

...is tough and gummy.

Over-cooked. (Follow directions carefully. Timing is especially important when making jelly.)

Not enough sugar was used. (Mixture had to be reduced in volume by boiling and so was over-cooked.)

...has mold form under the paraffin.

Seal was not good. (Use a thin layer of paraffin rather than a thick one. A thin one is a little flexible and will maintain a seal whereas a thick layer can easily be separated from the glass of the jar. When the jelly is exposed to air, mold can grow. Do not eat jelly that has visible mold because the tendrils of the mold can extend far down into the jar even though the mold appears to only be on the surface.)

MEAT

...color of uncooked meat looks "off".

Caused by over-long or improper storage. (Darkening of meat is caused by exposure to oxygen.)

...uncooked meat has an "off" odor.

Not fresh. (If in doubt, don't use it.)

...surface of uncooked meat looks dry.

Can be caused by freezer burn when meat is not properly wrapped and is exposed to cold dry air of the freezer for an extended time. (Raw meat that is frozen should be carefully wrapped and sealed. If you use heavy-duty foil, be sure to press all of the air pockets out. The paper that supermarket meat departments use to wrap meat in is not suitable for freezing the meat.)

...is tough when cooked.

Probably wrong cut of meat was used for cooking method chosen. (Leaner cuts, or meat from older animals need moisture added while cooking. Braising is a good way to cook less-than-tender cuts.)

Possibly the meat was not adequately aged. (Aging brings a certain amount of tenderizing to the meat. Meat purchased through a commercial meat outlet is almost always aged before it is sold.)

Broiled meat

...doesn't brown on outside but is cooked internally.

Surface of meat was not dried before cooking. (Always blot the surfaces of raw meat before broiling or searing. The meat must be dry or a layer of steam forms at the surface which makes it difficult for the meat to brown.)

...browns on outside but not cooked inside.

Broiled too near the heat source. (The thicker the piece of meat, the further it must be from the heat source to cook properly. Consult your manufacture's instruction book or a handbook such as my *The Cook's Book of Essential Information* for full information.)

...browned and cooked internally but very dry.

Cut of meat was too lean for good broiling. (It is usually the fat marbling that makes the meat tender, leaner cuts can be tenderized by marinating or using a commercial meat tenderizer.)

Meat was punctured often during cooking while turning or testing. (Rather that using a fork to turn the meat, use tongs.)

Could simply be over-cooked because the cut was too thin to broil well.

...edges curl.

If edge of meat is fat, it should be scored before cooking. (To "score" means to cut perpendicularly through the fat to the meat. You do this because as the fat cooks it shrinks and without scoring this shrinking will cause the meat to curl.)

Roasted meat

...is tough.

Usually because wrong cut has been chosen for the method used. (Dry roasting requires a piece that is not too lean. Braise leaner cuts by using a small amount of liquid and cooking in a tightly covered container.)

Meat may also simply be over-cooked. (Use a meat thermometer to get best results when cooking meat no matter what method you are using.)

...shrinks from original size.

Oven temperature was too high for roasting and meat juices have evaporated. (Most beef, lamb, and veal are roasted in the 300-325 degree Fahrenheit range; pork should be cooked with a little more heat [up to 350 degrees], smaller turkeys can be cooked at 350 but larger birds should be cooked at 325. Check a table of cooking times and temperatures for exact information.)

...is dry.

Oven temperature was too high for roasting. (Be sure that your oven heats to the temperature set on your oven thermostat and not higher.)

...is too well done.

Using a meat thermometer will assure that internal temperature is what it should be for meat cooked the way you would like it. (Without a meat thermometer, be sure correct weight of roast is used when estimating cooking time.)

Meat continues to "cook" after being removed from the oven. (Ideally it should be served in about 15-20 minutes after coming from the oven.)

...falls apart when sliced.

Cut too soon after removing from oven. (Allow the roast to "rest" about 10 to 15 minutes before slicing. This allows the meat to equalize in temperature and "solidify" for easy cutting.)

MERINGUE ON PIES

...shrinks from pie shell.

Meringue "floats" away from the pie shell. (Make sure meringue is anchored by touching the shell all the way around.)

...is tough.

Meringue was over-cooked. (Probably because oven temperature was too high.)

..."weeps".

Pie filling was cold before meringue was added. (Filling should still be no cooler that room temperature before covering with meringue.)

Sugar was not completely dissolved in the egg whites. (Start adding sugar as soon as the whites are frothy and beat until they will hold a stiff peak.)

Under-cooked. (Meringues have to be completely cooked to hold up well. Place the meringue on the filling, and bake at 400 degrees Fahrenheit for 8 to 10 minutes.)

MERINGUE SHELLS

...are sticky, not dry and firm.

Too much sugar for the amount of egg white. (Use large eggs as most recipes are based on using them. Measure sugar carefully.)

Egg whites were not beaten long enough. (Beat until stiff peaks form when beaters are lifted.)

Shells taken from oven too soon. (Let them remain in the oven until they are completely cool.)

The weather was too humid. (Meringues are weather-sensitive and will turn out best on a dry day.)

MUFFINS

...are shaped unevenly.

Fill muffin pans only 1/2 to 2/3's full and resist the temptation to add just that last little bit of batter. (Muffin cups that are too full will simply run over and make a mess.)

Oven temperature is too high. (The outside of the batter bakes first and the rest is forced out as it expands. The result is a cracked top and uneven shape.)

...have "tunnels"

The batter was too dry. (Too much flour or too little liquid can cause this. Keep proportions correct.)

The batter was mixed too much. (Make a depression in the center of the dry ingredients and add the liquid/egg mixture all at once. Mix only until the dry ingredients are moistened. Don't beat the batter.)

Muffins were baked to long or at too high a temperature. (Always use a preheated oven for best results.)

...don't raise as high as you would like.

If you do not use paper liners, grease only the bottom of the muffin cups so that the batter can cling to the un-greased sides of the cup while it bakes. To remove simply run a sharp, thin knife around the cup.

ONIONS

...mold quickly.

Stored with potatoes. (The onions absorb moisture from the potatoes and can quickly mold. Store onions separately in a cool dry place in a mesh bag or basket so that air can circulate. Best not to store in a plastic bag because air cannot circulate.)

PASTA

...sticks together.

Not enough water was used to cook the pasta. (Use no less than 4 quarts of water for each pound of uncooked pasta... Italian cooks often use 6 quarts to a pound of pasta.)

Water was not boiling when pasta was added. (Water has to be in a rolling boil for best results.)

No oil was added to water. (A tablespoon or two of olive oil added to the already boiling water will keep the pasta from sticking together. Oil will also keep the water from foaming over.)

...falls apart.

If it is homemade pasta, probably all-purpose flour was used. (For best results use semolina flour.)

Over-cooked. (Cook only until al dente, tender when you bite into it.)

PICKLES

...are shriveled.

In initial stages of making the pickles too much salt, vinegar, or sugar was used in the brine. (Start with greater dilutions in the brine to allow the produce to absorb it slowly and not give up its natural vegetable juice into the brine.)

Over-cooking. (Follow directions carefully.)

...are hollow.

Cucumbers were not solid. (Cut through a sample or two to make sure the produce is worth spending the time and money to preserve.)

Cucumbers were kept too long before pickling. (The less time between picking and pickling, the better.)

Brine was not the right proportion. (Follow recipe carefully.)

...soft, slippery texture.

Do not use pickles that have a soft or slippery texture. This is usually caused by bacterial action; the pickles are not "pickled" and bacteria are able to invade them to cause spoilage. (Common causes are; improper seal, not enough salt or acid in brine, or under-cooking.)

Can also be caused by enzyme action. (If blossoms are not entirely removed from cucumbers before pickling, softening may result.)

...turn dark.

Most often caused from using either iodized salt or using ground spices. (Use kosher or canning salt and whole spices.)

Can also be caused by hard water in the brine or over-cooking the pickles. (If your tap water is particularly hard, consider using distilled water for making pickles.)

PIE DOUGH

...is sticky and hard to roll out.

Too much water was added to the flour-shortening combination. (Add iced water only a tablespoonful at a time and gently mix until the dough will just hold together.)

Dough is too warm. (Use a pastry blender to combine flour and shortening instead of your hands. Chill the dough in the refrigerator.)

...breaks apart as it is rolled.

Dough is too cold. (Do not over-chill before rolling.)

Too much flour. (Be sure the proportion between flour and shortening are correct, or add a little more iced water.)

PIE CRUST

...is hard or tough.

Too much water has been added. (Excess water can cause a variety of problems. Experience is the best teacher in learning when just enough has been added.)

Not enough shortening. (Usual proportions are 1/3 cup shortening to each cup of flour. It is tempting to cut down on calories by reducing the shortening quantity but the result will be disappointing.)

Dough was handled too much. (Roll in one direction at a time, and roll out only until desired thickness is reached. Handle the dough as little as possible.)

Too much flour was used as dough was rolled out. (Use only enough to keep dough from sticking as it is rolled. You might consider buying a pastry cloth and cover for your rolling pin to minimize sticking.)

Oven was not preheated or oven temperature was too low. (Pie shells require 450 degree Fahrenheit temperature. Without adequate heat they tend to dry out rather than bake.)

...is tender rather than flaky.

Butter or soft margarine was used instead of shortening. (Shortening or lard are the best fats to use if you want flaky pie crust. Some recipes call for other fats, including oil, but the result will be different.)

...bakes unevenly.

Heat is not reaching the pie pan equally. (Foil on the oven rack or baking the pie on a cookie sheet can cause this effect.)

...shrinks in the pan as it bakes.

Too much water was used. (The water evaporates and the other ingredients contract.)

Too much shortening was used. (The proportion among flour, shortening and iced water is very important.)

Dough was stretched to fit pan. (Dough should fit in pan loosely.)

...unfilled crust puffs up and becomes bumpy and bubbly.

Crust was not adequately pricked before baking. (Use a table fork and pierce the unbaked crust all over, especially around the sides and in the bend where the bottom and sides meet. For most satisfactory results, don't hold back on this.)

Oven temperature was not high enough. (Pie crusts need a 450 degree Fahrenheit oven to bake properly. Check oven temperature with an oven thermometer.)

Shell not weighted down while baking. (Place a layer of dry beans in the shell for the first half of the baking time, remove to finish baking the shell.)

FILLED PIE

...has a soggy bottom crust.

Pie shell and/or filling were warm when combined. (Chill both the filling and the pie shell before putting together.)

Bottom crust needs to be "sealed". (Lightly beat an egg white and spread a thin layer over the bottom crust before adding the filling.)

PIE FILLING

...is too thin.

If thickened with cornstarch, could be because too much sugar was used, filling was over-cooked, or there were too many acid ingredients in the filling.

If thickened with tapioca, not enough tapioca was used.

If thickened with flour, too much sugar, not enough flour, or too many acidic ingredients in the filling.

...is too thick and sticky.

Too much thickener was used, particularly possible when using tapioca or flour.

...boils over and runs out of pie.

Too much filling was used. (It is better to leave a little in the mixing bowl than to have it run over and make a mess of your entire oven.)

Top was not well-sealed to bottom crust. (Make sure that the edge is well crimped and sealed.)

No slits were cut in the top crust. (As the filling heats, steam is created and has to have someplace to escape. A few slits or a decorative cut-out in the top crust takes care of the problem.)

POTATOES

...turn greenish colored on the outside.

Stored in too much light. (Potatoes should be stored in a dark place. Green portions and sprouts should be cut off before cooking the potato.)

...taste too sweet.

Stored in the refrigerator. (The cold damp air of the refrigerator turns the starch in potatoes to sugar which affects both the flavor and the texture. Potatoes should be stored in a cool, dry and dark place.)

...darken when cooked.

Stored in the refrigerator. (When the starch is converted to sugar, it can cause the potato to darken as it cooks.)

...mold quickly.

Stored in the refrigerator. (Dampness of refrigerator air causes potatoes to mold quickly.)

French fries

...greasy and limp.

Oil was not hot enough before potatoes were introduced. (Use a deep fat thermometer to check the temperature of the oil and make sure it is as hot as it should be for French fries, usually about 370 degrees Fahrenheit.)

Too many potatoes were put into the fryer at one time so the temperature of the oil was lowered. (Add only as many as you can comfortably add without reducing the temperature of the oil. The potatoes will cook more quickly and better if you do.)

Potato strips were piled up together to drain. (Drain in a single layer on a cooling rack or an absorbent paper towel.)

...brown too quickly.

Oil was too hot. (Potatoes brown on outside but are not completely cooked throughout.)

Starch on potato surface cooked first. (Place cut potato strips into a bowl of iced water to remove excess starch. Drain well and dry on paper towels before frying.)

Mashed potatoes

...are lumpy.

Potatoes were not cooked enough. (Potatoes have to be very tender to mash properly.)

Cold milk was added to the potatoes. (Warm the milk and melt the butter before adding to improve smoothness.)

RICE

...is sticky instead of fluffy.

Rice was over-cooked. (Check the rice periodically after about 20 minutes. When cooked it will be tender but still firm.)

Rice was stirred while cooking. (This disrupts the starch on the surface of the rice and causes it to clump together.)

"Wrong" kind of rice was used. (Some rices such as Italian arborio and some rices from south-east Asia are designed to stick together. Don't be surprised when they do. For fluffy rice use either brown, white, or converted.)

Too much water was used. (Follow directions regarding the amount of water as it varies among the various kinds of rice. To dry off the final bit of steam, crumple a paper towel and place it on top of the cooked rice and replace the lid on the pan. Leave it for about 10 minutes.)

...is tough.

Not cooked enough. (Sometimes happens when cooking brown rice or a short grained rice as they take a little longer than other rices to cook. Taste the rice and then cook some more if not tender.)

SAUCES

...egg-based sauce separates.

Oil added to quickly. (Hollandaise and mayonnaise are both susceptible to this. Add the oil or melted butter in a very thin stream while beating constantly.)

...Hollandaise is too thick.

Thin with a little water.

...Hollandaise is too thin.

Not enough acid in the mixture. (The balance among oil, eggs, and lemon or vinegar is critical.)

To thicken a thin sauce try this. In a separate bowl, whip together a tablespoon of thin hollandaise and a teaspoon of lemon juice. Beat well until it thickens. Add another tablespoon of sauce and beat again. Continue to add small amounts of sauce and beat the mixture until all of the think sauce has been thickened.

...cornstarch thickened sauce thins out.

Over-cooked. (Cook cornstarch thickened sauces only until thick and then remove from heat. Over-cooking will result in the sauce thinning out again.)

...arrowroot thickened sauce thins out.

Has been allowed to boil. (Sauces thickened with arrowroot should not be brought to a boil.)

...flour thickened sauce is too thin.

Not enough flour was used. (Check proportion of flour to liquid.)

Acidic food added to sauce. (This can cause sauce to thin out.)

SEASONINGS

...Dish is too salty.

There are several suggested ways to remedy this, sometimes they work adequately and sometimes not.

If the dish has just started cooking, add more ingredients and/or liquid to lower the proportion of salt in the finished product.

If the dish can cook some more, add chunks of potato, cook and then remove the potatoes before serving.

Add a small amount of sugar or vinegar. This is a last resort and will change the flavor of the dish but if you want to give it a try, you probably have nothing to lose.

If you are using condensed canned soup in a recipe, be very careful how much, if any, additional salt you add because those soups are quite high in salt.

...Dish doesn't have enough flavor.

Herbs or spices used are too old. (All foods have a shelf life. Ground herbs and spices last for about a year. Whole spices and dried herb leaves will last longer but not forever. It is better to buy smaller amounts of seasoning more often than large amounts only rarely.)

Fresh herbs were used instead of dried. (Some recipes do not specify whether to use dry or fresh herbs. Usually it is safe to assume that dried herbs are meant. Fresh herbs can be substituted at about 3 to 1, 3 units of fresh for 1 unit of dried, but it is important to taste as you go along.)

Dried herbs and/or spices had not been stored in a good location. (All spices, herbs, and other seasoning and flavorings should be stored in a cool, dry, dark place for longest shelf life.)

Too much liquid used. (The seasonings are spread out over too much volume.

...Dish is too highly seasoned.

Recipe was mis-read or ingredients were mis-measured. (Most seasonings are quite potent so be careful about what you add... because once added it is just about impossible to take them out again. It is not a good idea to measure seasonings over the bowl that you are mixing the dish in... if you over-fill the measuring spoon, you don't want the excess to go into the dish.)

The liquid has cooked down too much. (The seasonings are concentrated in too small a volume.)

SHRIMP

...Texture is tough.

Shrimp was over-cooked. (Cook only until pink in color.)

...has a black line down the back.

This is called a "vein" but is actually part of the shrimp's digestive system. (It should be removed. Use a sharp knife with a thin blade and remove the black line under running water.)

VEGETABLES

...are too soft and mushy.

Vegetables were over-cooked. (Don't let them stand in hot water or over steam after they are cooked because cooking will continue. Check vegetables periodically while they are cooking to test for tenderness.)

...are tough in texture.

Vegetables were probably too mature when they were cooked. (Younger produce cooks quickly and is more tender.)

...change color when cooked.

White vegetables can turn yellowish in color if they are cooked in hard water. (Try adding a little lemon juice or vinegar to the cooking water.)

Red vegetables can turn blue or greenish in color if they are cooked in hard water. (Add a little lemon juice or vinegar to the cooking water.)

INDEX

Z

ORDER FORM

SUMNER HOUSE PRESS
2527 West Kennewick Avenue
Suite 190
Kennewick, Washington, 99336

Please indicate the number of copies of each title you would like.

____THE COOK'S BOOK OF™ ESSENTIAL INFORMATION $9.95   _____

____THE COOK'S BOOK OF™ INDISPENSABLE IDEAS $9.95   _____

____THE COOK'S BOOK OF™ UNCOMMON RECIPES $9.95   _____

TOTAL ORDER _____

Washington residents please add 7.8% sales tax. _____

Shipping charge on order $1.50

Enclosed is my check or money order for _____

Your complete satisfaction is guaranteed.

Name: _____

Mailing Address: _____

City/State/ZIP: _____

A Great Gift Idea ... for Birthdays ... for Weddings ... for Anniversaries ... for Graduates ... for Christmas ... for Any Occasion for Anyone Who Cooks

SUMNER HOUSE PRESS
2527 West Kennewick Avenue
Suite 190
Kennewick, Washington 99336

I would like to order copies of the books noted below to be sent to the people whose address I have listed. I have enclosed $9.95 for each book plus $1.50 to cover shipping and handling for the entire order. (For shipments to Washington state addresses, please add 7.8% sales tax for each copy.)

THE COOK'S BOOK OF™ UNCOMMON RECIPES
THE COOK'S BOOK OF™ ESSENTIAL INFORMATION
THE COOKS BOOK OF™ INDISPENSABLE IDEAS

Book Title: _____

Name: _____

Mailing Address: _____

City/State/ZIP: _____

Ship to receive by (date): _____

Gift card should say: _____

Book Title: _____

Name: _____

Mailing Address: _____

City/State/ZIP _____

Ship to receive by (date): _____

Gift card should say: _____

My name is: _____

Mailing Address: _____

City/State/ZIP _____

YOUR COMPLETE SATISFACTION IS GUARANTEED!

ORDER FORM

SUMNER HOUSE PRESS
2527 West Kennewick Avenue
Suite 190
Kennewick, Washington, 99336

Please indicate the number of copies of each title you would like.

_____THE COOK'S BOOK OF™ ESSENTIAL INFORMATION $9.95   _____

_____THE COOK'S BOOK OF™ INDISPENSABLE IDEAS $9.95   _____

_____THE COOK'S BOOK OF™ UNCOMMON RECIPES $9.95   _____

TOTAL ORDER _____

Washington residents please add 7.8% sales tax. _____

Shipping charge on order ___ $1.50 ___

Enclosed is my check or money order for _____

Your complete satisfaction is guaranteed.

Name: _____

Mailing Address: _____

City/State/ZIP: _____

A Great Gift Idea ... for Birthdays ... for Weddings ... for Anniversaries ... for Graduates ... for Christmas ... for Any Occasion for Anyone Who Cooks

SUMNER HOUSE PRESS
2527 West Kennewick Avenue
Suite 190
Kennewick, Washington 99336

I would like to order copies of the books noted below to be sent to the people whose address I have listed. I have enclosed $9.95 for each book plus $1.50 to cover shipping and handling for the entire order. (For shipments to Washington state addresses, please add 7.8% sales tax for each copy.)

THE COOK'S BOOK OF™ UNCOMMON RECIPES
THE COOK'S BOOK OF™ ESSENTIAL INFORMATION
THE COOKS BOOK OF™ INDISPENSABLE IDEAS

Book Title: _____

Name: _____

Mailing Address: _____

City/State/ZIP: _____

Ship to receive by (date): _____

Gift card should say: _____

Book Title: _____

Name: _____

Mailing Address: _____

City/State/ZIP _____

Ship to receive by (date): _____

Gift card should say: _____

My name is: _____

Mailing Address: _____

City/State/ZIP _____

YOUR COMPLETE SATISFACTION IS GUARANTEED!

ORDER FORM

SUMNER HOUSE PRESS
2527 West Kennewick Avenue
Suite 190
Kennewick, Washington, 99336

Please indicate the number of copies of each title you would like.

_____THE COOK'S BOOK OF™ ESSENTIAL INFORMATION $9.95   _____

_____THE COOK'S BOOK OF™ INDISPENSABLE IDEAS $9.95   _____

_____THE COOK'S BOOK OF™ UNCOMMON RECIPES $9.95   _____

TOTAL ORDER _____

Washington residents please add 7.8% sales tax. _____

Shipping charge on order ___$1.50___

Enclosed is my check or money order for _____

Your complete satisfaction is guaranteed.

Name: _____

Mailing Address: _____

City/State/ZIP: _____

A Great Gift Idea ... for Birthdays ... for Weddings ... for Anniversaries ... for Graduates ... for Christmas ... for Any Occasion for Anyone Who Cooks

SUMNER HOUSE PRESS
2527 West Kennewick Avenue
Suite 190
Kennewick, Washington 99336

I would like to order copies of the books noted below to be sent to the people whose address I have listed. I have enclosed $9.95 for each book plus $1.50 to cover shipping and handling for the entire order. (For shipments to Washington state addresses, please add 7.8% sales tax for each copy.)

THE COOK'S BOOK OF™ UNCOMMON RECIPES
THE COOK'S BOOK OF™ ESSENTIAL INFORMATION
THE COOKS BOOK OF™ INDISPENSABLE IDEAS

Book Title: _____

Name: _____

Mailing Address: _____

City/State/ZIP: _____

Ship to receive by (date): _____

Gift card should say: _____

Book Title: _____

Name: _____

Mailing Address: _____

City/State/ZIP _____

Ship to receive by (date): _____

Gift card should say: _____

_____

My name is: _____

Mailing Address: _____

City/State/ZIP _____

YOUR COMPLETE SATISFACTION IS GUARANTEED!

ORDER FORM

SUMNER HOUSE PRESS
2527 West Kennewick Avenue
Suite 190
Kennewick, Washington, 99336

Please indicate the number of copies of each title you would like.

_____THE COOK'S BOOK OF™ ESSENTIAL INFORMATION $9.95   _____

_____THE COOK'S BOOK OF™ INDISPENSABLE IDEAS $9.95   _____

_____THE COOK'S BOOK OF™ UNCOMMON RECIPES $9.95   _____

TOTAL ORDER _____

Washington residents please add 7.8% sales tax. _____

Shipping charge on order ___ $1.50 ___

Enclosed is my check or money order for _____

Your complete satisfaction is guaranteed.

Name: _____

Mailing Address: _____

City/State/ZIP: _____

A Great Gift Idea ... for Birthdays ... for Weddings ... for Anniversaries ... for Graduates ... for Christmas ... for Any Occasion for Anyone Who Cooks

SUMNER HOUSE PRESS

2527 West Kennewick Avenue
Suite 190
Kennewick, Washington 99336

I would like to order copies of the books noted below to be sent to the people whose address I have listed. I have enclosed $9.95 for each book plus $1.50 to cover shipping and handling for the entire order. (For shipments to Washington state addresses, please add 7.8% sales tax for each copy.)

THE COOK'S BOOK OF™ UNCOMMON RECIPES
THE COOK'S BOOK OF™ ESSENTIAL INFORMATION
THE COOKS BOOK OF™ INDISPENSABLE IDEAS

Book Title:_____

Name: _____

Mailing Address: _____

City/State/ZIP: _____

Ship to receive by (date): ____

Gift card should say: _____

Book Title: _____

Name: _____

Mailing Address: _____

City/State/ZIP _____

Ship to receive by (date): _____

Gift card should say: _____

My name is: _____

Mailing Address: _____

City/State/ZIP _____

YOUR COMPLETE SATISFACTION IS GUARANTEED!